Successful School

Transition

Practical ideas and workshops to
support children changing from primary
to secondary school

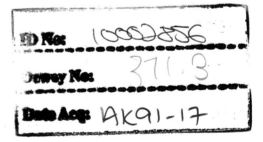
Ainsley Dawrent

Permission to photocopy

This book contains materials which may be reproduced by photocopier or other means for use by the purchaser. The permission is granted on the understanding that these copies will be used within the educational establishment of the purchaser. The book and all its contents remain copyright. Copies may be made without reference to the publisher or the licensing scheme for the making of photocopies operated by the Publishers' Licensing Agency.

Dedication

To my best teachers, my parents Dorothy and Terry Walker, with love.

Acknowledgements

Thanks to the many who helped with this book.

Everyone in the London Borough of Newham: head teachers and staff of North Beckton Primary; St Stephen's, Tollgate; Sheringham Juniors; Salisbury Primary; Britannia Village Primary; Little Ilford Secondary; Eastlea Community; Kingsford Community, Stratford; Brampton Manor.

Attendees of the Y6/7 transition network meetings; borough consultants: Richard Ray, Caroline Stone, Steve Wright (for consultant lessons), Linda Potticary, John Mills, Liz Floyd, Maria Maher, Pamela Clarke, Yvonne Collyer and Myannah Saunders; the wonderful teachers on the Y6 and Y7 English transition units working parties, P4C Wiz Lisa Naylor at Gallions Primary.

All schools and borough support staff (especially Laura, Marion, Karen, Anne and Dave).

Fellow transition specialists: Hilary Belden at Ealing LEA for project ideas, Peter Copcutt at Camden LEA for a draft Y6–Y7 Transition Audit used in schools and the base of my own audit in this book.

Hackney primaries for SPIQe development work, especially Harrington Hill; Carol Greenaway, Educational Psychologist; Hallfield Juniors and Wilberforce Primary in Westminster, London.

Special thanks to Her Biz in Newham, my coach Moira Bailey (who asked 'So, why exactly are you delaying writing this book?') and Her Biz NLP Practitioner trainer Jane Lewis; to Mike and Lucy Fleetham for encouragement and advice; Corin Redsell of LDA, a patient editor used to nutty writers; and my wacky and wise friends: Anita, Angus and Anne, E and E, Jayne, Vicky, Pam, Linda and Dona. Plus BJ and CP and their tribes. To Philip at Anglo-American Books and Viv/John at the Newham Bookshop, for wonderful books and no space in my flat.

Lastly to all the children I've taught and who have taught me, especially 6D at Wilberforce Primary, Westminster, in 2003–4 who gave me the ideas for the Head/Heart/Gut Instinct theme. May you be the best you can be, at all times.

Successful School Transition

MT10787

ISBN-13: 978 1 85503 435 8

© Ainsley Dawrent

Illustrations © Jorge Santillan

All rights reserved

First published 2008

Printed in the UK for LDA

Abbeygate House, East Road, Cambridge, CB1 1DB, UK

▷ Contents

▷ 1. Introduction

When planning for a year, plant corn.
When planning for a decade, plant trees.
When planning for life, train and educate people.

Chinese proverb

This is a practical, hands-on book that I have written to help fellow practitioners concerned with primary to secondary transition. I want to share the lessons I've learned and the ideas I've generated when working in this area. It's a book about the head, heart and gut instinct issues of transition for pupils. It is adaptable for transition from primary to middle schools. Throughout it includes guidance for use with children with special needs.

After nine years of teaching children in upper Key Stage 2, especially those in Year 6 (Y6), in challenging schools in five different London boroughs, I was employed by the London Borough of Newham as their Year 6–7 transition consultant to run a two-year project. I grabbed the opportunity because I wanted to answer some of the questions I had about the process of transition that the pupils I taught went through, and about its effectiveness. How did different schools handle this process? What was it like for children to move from small primary schools to larger secondary schools? How could transition be developed and improved so that primary and secondary teachers learned from each other how to help children become the best they could be?

From 2004 to 2006, I worked in six primary schools and five secondary schools in the borough. During this time, I organised and ran network meetings on transition and a transition conference, led staff training in the project schools, and helped nurture various cross-phase teaching and learning projects. The consultants, support staff, teachers and pupils in Newham made all the aspects of this project possible. It is their wisdom and the lessons we learned together that I shall share with you in this book.

It was through these activities and pupil-voice research that I developed the idea of head, heart and gut instinct workshops, which form the core of this book. The head workshops help pupils develop the way they think. The heart workshops focus on issues concerning friendship and enhancing social skills. Finally, the gut instinct workshops are concerned with being safe and how to integrate successfully at secondary (or middle) school. Chapters 3, 4 and 5 of this book explain these workshops, which can be run in Year 6 prior to transition, in Year 7 (Y7) during transition or, best of all, as a joint project involving both years. They can also be used for transition to middle school.

By developing effective cross-phase links between schools, you will go a long way towards reducing the academic dip that occurs over the course of Year 7. Such liaison enables secondary staff to become aware of the level of discipline and independence shown by pupils at primary level, which will help inform behaviour policies and raise expectations. Visits that involve secondary teachers participating in literacy and mathematics lessons, as opposed to observing, is empowering for both visiting and host teachers. Finding ways to work together will energise all the teaching staff involved.

The materials in this book aim to help teachers from both sending and receiving schools overcome the fears that they have about transition, which they admit to rarely. Primary teachers may be concerned about visiting a school where they are no longer the tallest inhabitants and the learning moves beyond level 7 of the National Curriculum. Secondary teachers may be quite anxious about being in a school full of small children, with whom they are not used to interacting – although this may seem odd, it was a real fear that I encountered several times.

Better liaison will also help to debunk myths often expressed about pupils of transition age. Some secondary-school teachers may claim that primary-school children don't really operate at level 4/5. On occasion, it may be the teaching and learning in Year 7 that needs to stretch. Secondary departments may re-teach much of Year 6 in Year 7 (and middle schools may do much the same thing). Secondary teaching staff need access to primary-school pupil records and work samples. Using the materials in this book as part of cross-phase learning will help teachers from both sides of the transition process grow in understanding of the skills of their colleagues.

Senior management in primary and secondary schools must value and build links to ensure successful transition. Examine how timetabling in secondary – where lessons often last 50 minutes and start/ end times vary from primary – can be adapted so teachers can visit primaries. Similarly, it's difficult for primary teachers to visit secondaries unless given time to do so.

View the final report at www.secondary.newham.gov.uk by selecting secondary networks, followed by Building More Bridges: The Newham Y6–Y7 Transition Project 2004–2006 End of Project Report.

What ideas underpin primary to secondary transition?

Transfer and Transitions in the Middle Years of Schooling (7–14) by Maurice Galton, John Gray and Jean Ruddock (publication details are on page 96) identified five 'bridges' that pupils have to cross to make an effective primary to secondary school transition. These bridges are as follows.

Bureaucratic bridge – how is information transferred?

This covers liaison between primary and secondary schools at borough / local authority level, and is concerned with the effective transfer of records between school offices. Special needs records may be included in this transfer, although there should be specific arrangements for statemented pupils, involving an annual review attended by both schools, and a more detailed, intensive and personalised induction to their secondary school for the child. The role of learning mentors as a means to support vulnerable pupils through transition is part of this bridge.

Social and emotional bridge – parents and pupils prepared

This bridge concerns social skills, friendship and being safe, and is of prime importance to children. Friendship issues are covered in the Chapter 4 workshops, and safety in the Chapter 5 workshops.

Curriculum bridge – curriculum/learning continuity

Subject continuity and eliminating the dip in learning constitutes the prime transition bridge in terms of a child's academic development. While pupils recognise the importance of this area, they are more concerned with the social and emotional bridge. Cross-phase teaching and effective subject-based transition units can help here. The head workshops in Chapter 3, along with the introductory workshop in Chapter 2, will focus on this area.

Pedagogy bridge – continuation of teaching pedagogy and practice

This focuses on *how* children learn, rather than on *what* they learn. The workshops in Chapter 3 cover this aspect. This work focuses on the ways children think about how they are intelligent, how they process ideas and the things they like to do.

Management of learning bridge – children own their learning

How can children 'own' their learning, involve their parents or carers and become part of their new school? Finding answers to these questions underpins all the workshops. Successful secondary or middle school induction and orientation activities must focus on this bridge.

How is my school dealing with the five bridges?

Chapter 6 sets out a transition audit you can use in your school. This will help you assess your current provision and highlight areas of development. It presents sample transition policies to enable you to target your interventions and compare your school's transition focus with other ways of working.

I hope you, your colleagues and the children with whom you work will enjoy the activities in the book, and that these will support successful transition.

2. Head, heart and gut instinct introductory workshop

Confusion is the hallmark of transition.
To rebuild both your inner and outer world is a major project.

Anne Grant, writer and consultant on grief issues

The thinking behind the workshop

This workshop began as a sample pupil-voice questionnaire I developed with my last Year 6 class at Wilberforce Primary, in Queens Park, London, in 2004. Its aim was to clarify their main worries about moving to secondary school.

I found that pupils were more focused on the heart (emotional and social) and gut instinct (safety) issues of moving across phases than the head areas of teaching and learning. My subsequent work in primary to secondary transition highlighted the importance of getting all three areas right for pupils. The questionnaire was refined and used for pupil-voice research: the Year 6 version for pupils leaving in July, with a follow-up interview of the same pupils with the Year 7 version in November. It then also became the starting point for pupil transition workshops.

As such, it has been run in different ways, independently within KS2 and KS3 and also as a joint primary/ secondary project. Both models are presented to you to decide, given your school circumstances, which is more suitable for you.

Year 6 to Year 7 – What do you Think? (1 hour)
In a Year 6 (version A) or Year 7 (version B) class – using appropriate handout.

◗ Learning intention

Pupils can identify their areas of concern in transition to secondary school.

◗ Success criteria

Pupils can:

- discuss their concerns in each area with others, acknowledging what they have in common;
- segment their concerns into different areas (head / heart / gut instinct) to decide which are their priority areas;
- (done with partner secondary school) share concerns with Year 7 pupils and teachers.

◗ Resources

Photocopiables 1A for Year 6 (page 10) and 1B for Year 7 (page 11). Use Photocopiable 1B in PSHE or tutor group lessons in Year 7. Use both when the workshop is a cross-phase project involving primary to secondary transition co-ordinators with pupils. You will need one photocopiable for each pupil

A3 paper, coloured pencils

▷ Introduction to version A

Group pupils in mixed-ability pairs. Give each pupil a handout (Photocopiable 1A). Explain that they will be thinking and writing about their concerns for beginning Year 7 and how they will cope with them.

Paired sharing

Introduce the three sections in turn. After you introduce the first (head), encourage the pairs to discuss what they will write on their forms. They then fill in that part. Repeat for heart, and gut instinct.

▷ Whole-class discussion

Once all the sections are completed, the class share their responses. Use an interactive whiteboard (IWB) or a flipchart to record common issues in teaching and learning (head), friendship (heart) and safety (gut instinct). Ensure that all comments are respected. You may find that boys are initially less open than girls about issues to do with friendship and safety. After discussion, ask the pupils to review their own forms and use a different-coloured pencil to add any extra issues of concern to them that classmates have raised. Save the IWB screen or flipchart pages for future reference, along with the completed forms.

▷ Plenary

Ask the pupils to discuss in table groups the issues they have noted – head, heart, gut instinct – and also to consider what they know now that should help them deal with these issues and what they would like to learn about.

Record these discussion points yourself or get the groups to note them on A3 sheets of paper divided into the three sections: Head, Heart and Gut instinct.

Discuss what has been recorded, and tell them that these issues will be discussed and solutions developed in future workshops.

If working with a Year 7 group, use Photocopiable 1B and tailor your comments accordingly.

 ## Version B

This is a simple and effective cross-phase project, involving Year 7 staff and pupils.

Organise a group of Year 7 pupils (usually a maximum of 6 is workable) and secondary staff from a linked secondary school to attend your Year 6 workshop 1 (version A). I found that English and media staff were keen to be involved.

The session proceeds as previous, except that the Year 7 pupils move round the room with clipboards and digital or video cameras, noting pupils' concerns. In this initial lesson the Year 7 pupils do not feed back to the pupils. For example, if a Year 7 pupil hears a Year 6 pupil making a comment that they know is incorrect for their secondary school, or that they can answer, they do not respond but note the comment and response on their clipboard.

The Year 7 pupils attend to obtain ideas and concerns. They take these back to their school and do either of the following:

- Produce a brochure or some form of simple multi-media presentation answering the main concerns raised by Year 6 pupils. In a subsequent session, they present this to the pupils and answer questions.

- Invite some of the Year 6 pupils to their secondary school and prepare a presentation, jointly with the Year 6 children, to return and present at the primary school.

Both workshop models are highly effective. In one year of my project, the Year 7 pupils visited two primaries, took notes and pictures/videos, then returned a month later with a superb presentation on learning, socialising and school organisation issues. During the second year of the transition project, emboldened by the experience in the first year, the secondary media teacher suggested that Year 6 pupils (from the same two primaries) visit his school after the initial workshop and make a film covering the issues raised. This was completed within a month and the film was shown to children in the two primaries. It was also used by the secondary and primary teachers in a transition workshop for other teachers.

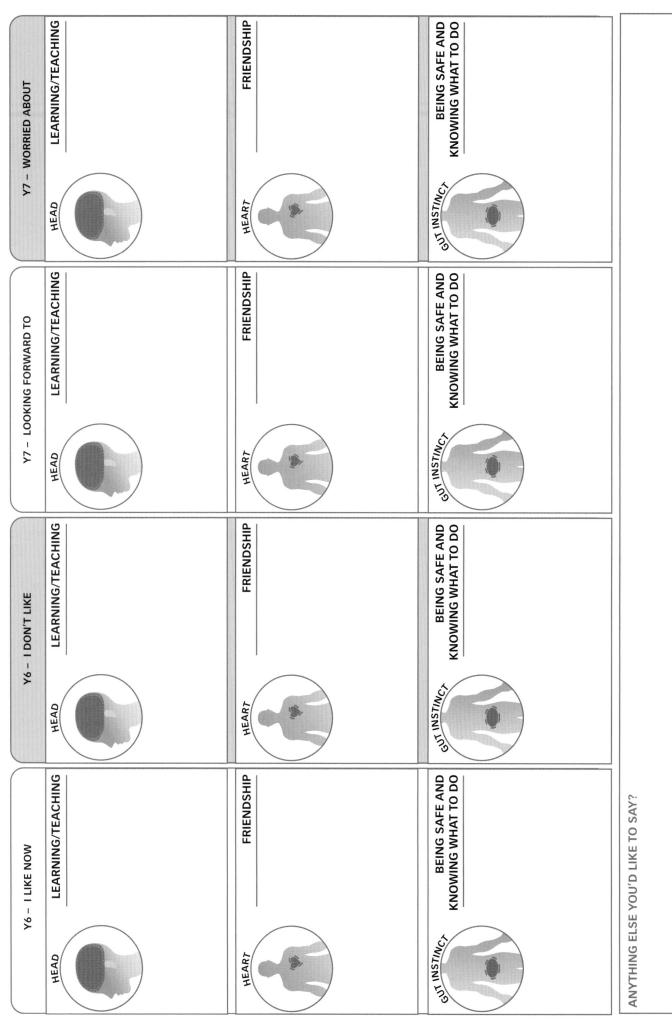

Y6 – I LIKE NOW

HEAD · LEARNING/TEACHING

HEART · FRIENDSHIP

GUT INSTINCT · BEING SAFE AND KNOWING WHAT TO DO

Y6 – I DON'T LIKE

HEAD · LEARNING/TEACHING

HEART · FRIENDSHIP

GUT INSTINCT · BEING SAFE AND KNOWING WHAT TO DO

Y7 – LOOKING FORWARD TO

HEAD · LEARNING/TEACHING

HEART · FRIENDSHIP

GUT INSTINCT · BEING SAFE AND KNOWING WHAT TO DO

Y7 – WORRIED ABOUT

HEAD · LEARNING/TEACHING

HEART · FRIENDSHIP

GUT INSTINCT · BEING SAFE AND KNOWING WHAT TO DO

ANYTHING ELSE YOU'D LIKE TO SAY?

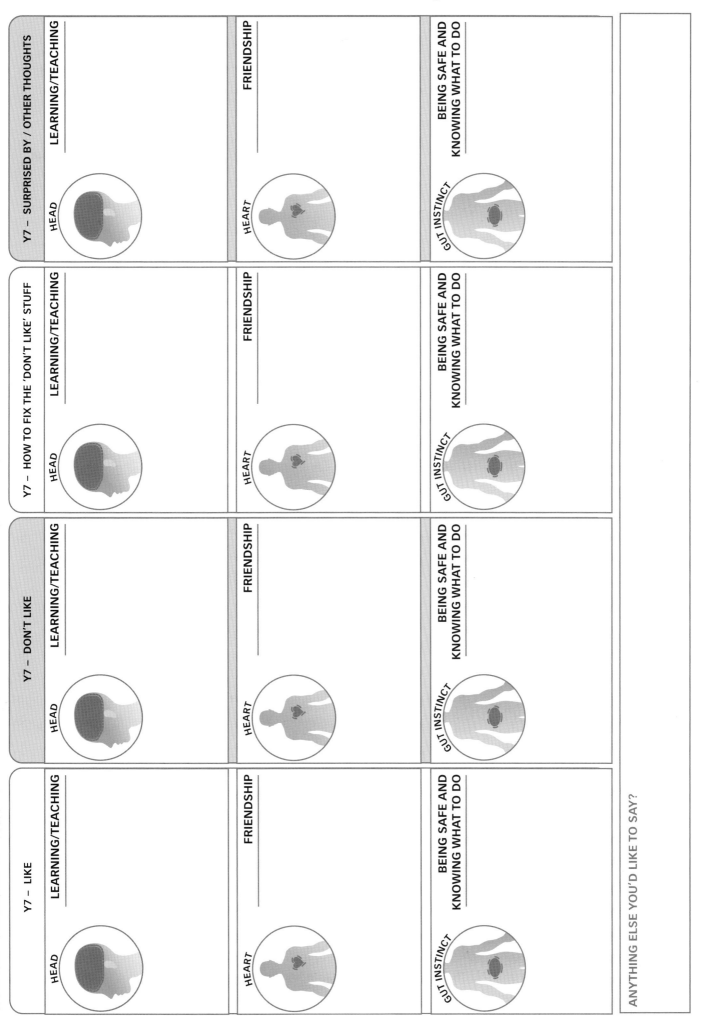

Y7 – SURPRISED BY / OTHER THOUGHTS

- HEAD — LEARNING/TEACHING
- HEART — FRIENDSHIP
- GUT INSTINCT — BEING SAFE AND KNOWING WHAT TO DO

Y7 – HOW TO FIX THE 'DON'T LIKE' STUFF

- HEAD — LEARNING/TEACHING
- HEART — FRIENDSHIP
- GUT INSTINCT — BEING SAFE AND KNOWING WHAT TO DO

Y7 – DON'T LIKE

- HEAD — LEARNING/TEACHING
- HEART — FRIENDSHIP
- GUT INSTINCT — BEING SAFE AND KNOWING WHAT TO DO

Y7 – LIKE

- HEAD — LEARNING/TEACHING
- HEART — FRIENDSHIP
- GUT INSTINCT — BEING SAFE AND KNOWING WHAT TO DO

ANYTHING ELSE YOU'D LIKE TO SAY?

We are told never to cross a bridge till we come to it, but this world is owned by people who have crossed bridges in their imagination far ahead of the crowd.

Anonymous

Pupils moving to another school are often so concerned about making friends (heart), and fitting in and being safe (gut instinct) in their new, larger schools, that they completely overlook the skills required to learn well in Year 7 and beyond.

Pupils need to know how they learn as well as how to have a positive attitude to learning. That is the focus of this chapter's workshops. It aims to equip your pupils to be independent learners in Year 6 and to transfer these skills to secondary school. You may wish to run these workshops early in Year 6. They could also be modified to use in Year 7 to assess the transition the pupils had made and for transition to middle schools.

Research has shown that the real issue of primary to secondary transfer is curriculum continuity. Secondary schools create problems for their pupils and teachers when they talk of Year 7 being a 'new start'. It is not. It is a continuation and development of the good teaching and learning of the primary school, not a repeat of the Year 6 curriculum. The main success of the Newham Year 6 to Year 7 transition project was in developing primary–secondary cross-phase teaching and learning projects, even tiny ones, that brought teachers together and enabled secondary teachers to discover the high quality of primary learning. When primary and secondary link-schools collaborate to team-teach some of these lessons they will increase their power and effectiveness.

Using your head workshops 2 and 3

Performance Monster and Learning Muscles: (2 hours each)

When I met my new Year 6 classes for the first time, I would say to the children: 'Point to who owns your learning.' I would then note who pointed to themselves and who pointed at me! Thereafter followed my Big Teacher Talk 101, explaining that their job in Year 6 was to become independent learners and that they were responsible for that learning. Teachers were not there to give them the answers, but to help them to ask questions and to equip them to find their own answers. This would mean making lots of mistakes and mistakes were OK. Not making mistakes meant they weren't challenging themselves to do more, to be the best they could be.

Subsequently, on reading the work of Carol Dweck (see References, page 96), I discovered that I'd hit the nail on the head. Effective learning is about having an internal locus of control (believing you control your life), and believing that you can keep learning and growing your intelligence. Dweck's research defined two views of intelligence.

1. Entity view of intelligence (Performance Monster)

Students with this view of intelligence:

- believe their intelligence is fixed and that fixed ability is what leads to success;

- want to perform well in specific learning situations (e.g. KS2 Year 6 tests) and are low risk-takers because failure – any failure – is seen as evidence of low intelligence;

- develop goals based on being best / avoiding failure – they may lack an internal locus of control;

- believe success happens because they have ability, failure occurs because that ability is fixed and can't be increased, and past or future success doesn't guarantee future success.

Dweck noted that 'praise for intelligence rather than effort creates vulnerability in high ability students that does not show up until they experience setbacks and failure'. When students believe that their intelligence is fixed, setbacks will happen in secondary school, if not in Year 6. This experience determines their approach to learning – above all, they avoid risk and making mistakes. They display helplessness when faced with difficult tasks or tasks that are just different from the pen and paper tasks they expect.

2. Incremental view of intelligence (Learning Muscles)

Students with this view:

- believe they can change and grow their intelligence, they can improve, and effort leads to success;

- enjoy challenges, even when the outcome makes them appear less smart; learning goals, persistence and mastering new skills are valued; they are always ready for the new challenge rather than repeating previous successes, avoiding risks;

- are happy making mistakes to learn; they own their learning.

Consider Assessment for Learning (AfL), with learning intentions, success criteria, peer- and self-marking and its formative assessment approach. All of this aims to build Learning Muscles, hence all the workshops in this book are designed to incorporate AfL strategies.

Performance Monster and Learning Muscles (2 hours)

❍ Learning intention

Pupils understand that they need to be responsible for their own learning to be successful students.

❍ Success criteria

Pupils:

- can identify blocks to owning their learning;
- can make mistakes without fear and explain why making mistakes is necessary for learning;
- recognise when they seek or avoid challenge;
- use practical exercises to develop their understanding of owning their learning;
- identify Learning Muscles and Performance Monsters.

❍ Resources

Photocopiable 2A (page 27), one for each pupil; Photocopiable 2B (page 28), one for each child; Photocopiable 2C (page 29), one for each pair; Photocopiable 2D (page 30), one for each pair; Post-it® notes, one for each child; pens or pencils

▷ Introduction

1. Give your pupils Photocopiable 2A. Assist special needs pupils by reading the text (or brief a teaching assistant to do so; insist they should not 'prime' pupils). Tell the pupils there are no right or wrong answers. They should note down what they themselves believe to be true as their answers, or what they prefer. The questionnaire should be completed quite quickly.

2. With the pupils in mixed-ability pairs, give each child a copy of Photocopiable 2B to complete, so they can determine their focus. Give them each a Post-it note to write down their orientation (P for performance; L for Learning); their marks total will reveal this. They will not yet know what it means. Take in the completed worksheets.

3. Hand out Photocopiable 2C, one to each pair. Lead a discussion on what the orientations mean.

4. Share the learning intention and success criteria (above) for this session with the pupils.

▷ Main activity

1. Hand out Photocopiable 2D (one per pair). Ask the pairs to note on their worksheet what's positive, negative and interesting about having a performance orientation to learning; then what's positive, negative and interesting about a learning orientation. In pairs, they discuss which is the more powerful approach for them.

2. Share ideas, recording them on an IWB or a flipchart. Save the ideas for the next session.

3. Discuss why the learning orientation approach will be more effective for them. Explain that for some areas of our lives we may have a performance orientation. Ask pupils to think of a subject area they think they're not good at and perhaps have given up on, one for which they think they have a fixed ability, so they don't try or risk making mistakes. How would having a learning orientation help them? Give your own example first, to start the discussion.

4. Do this 'imagining a turn' exercise, and discuss. If necessary, adapt this for children with special needs. Pupils in wheelchairs, or with physical disabilities, use their eyes or move their fingers. Children with balance problems can be seated in a chair. A teaching assistant may need to help a dyspraxic or hyperactive child.

a) Ask the pupils to move into an open area. Sit them on the floor. Stand at the front and state that you are going to give them a set of instructions to follow in silence.

b) Before they stand, demonstrate what you want them to do. Stand, your legs hip distance apart and straight, with your arms by your sides. Look ahead to find a spot on the wall on which to focus. Stretch one arm out straight ahead of you to point at that spot. Keep that arm up. Now turn your upper body, stretching and turning only at your waist, so you point that arm as far behind you as you can, noting the spot on the wall it points towards. Show the children you are not bending your legs and knees. Ask the pupils to stand, and talk them through the exercise from front to one side, then back round to the front.

c) Ask the children to sit down again on the floor cross-legged, close their eyes and picture in their minds what you are about to tell them. Say: 'Imagine you see this happening on a blue screen in front of you. See yourself stand up again, put your arm out, point to the same spot in front of you, but now when you turn to the side your waist is bendy and stretchy and easily, so easily, you turn further round. See this happening on the blue screen. Now see yourself coming back round to the front. See it happening in your mind, on a little blue screen. Now, open your eyes, stand up again in silence and do the same exercise again, in silence.'

d) The children stand up, again you model what to do, and they follow you, doing the same exercise.

▷ Plenary

The pupils sit on the floor. Ask how many were able to move round further the second time. Most pupils are able to move much further round. How? They've used their Learning Muscles. If they weren't able to move further, ask if there was a little voice saying it was silly. This is the Performance Monster, warning them against trying something new and taking a risk.

Ask the pupils to use thumbs up (green), sideways (amber) or downwards (red) to indicate to you and themselves which of the success criteria from page 14 they've met in this lesson and which need further work. Ask them to note in all their lessons when they use each approach to learning.

Discuss what they have learned.

Workshop 3

- ❍ Learning intention and success criteria

  As Workshop 2 (page 14).

- ❍ Resources

  Photocopiable 3A (page 31), one for each pupil; materials for main activities chosen by the pupils; pencils, paper and erasers

▷ Introduction

Ask the pupils to share what they know about the Performance Monster and Learning Muscles. Discuss the good/bad/interesting conclusions you reached in the last lesson, using the records you drew up with your class. Share the same learning intention and success criteria (page 14).

Let the pupils know that you're now going to use the skills needed to develop Learning Muscles.

▷ Main activity

Pupils choose a follow-up activity from these:

1. Design and make Learning Muscles and Performance Monster posters (art or ICT).

2. Devise, rehearse, then perform a TV advertisement for Learning Muscles or one against the Performance Monster. What do Learning Muscles look like? What is the Performance Monster?

3. Coaching exercise. Pick an area of their life in which the Performance Monster has limited them, find a classmate who has a Learning Muscle for that area and share. The Learning Muscle classmate finds one skill they can teach their partner. They talk about it, do it and then share it with the class. This could be done by using a PC, a sports skill, drawing, a reading skill.

▷ Plenary

Show the advertisements or video; display posters or digital pictures; share the coaching exercise.

Discuss what you've learned as a team about Learning Muscles. Develop buddy pairs for subjects in which pupils have a Performance Monster. Check the success criteria with thumbs up/across/down.

▷ Follow-up activity

Another way to enable pupils to enhance their Learning Muscles is to use ideas from Betty Edwards's *Drawing on the Right Side of the Brain* in a set of quick art workshops with your class. These teach pupils to draw what they see, not what they think they see.

In the first lesson, pair the pupils up. Each pair has a copy of Photocopiable 3A (page 31), pencils, an eraser and paper.

1. Draw your own hand, in detail (5 minutes). Sign and date your picture.

2. Take turns drawing the side profile of your partner (10 minutes each). Sign and date the picture.

These are the 'before' pictures.

Next, do these activities quickly, in a follow-up lesson.

1. Draw round the shape (5–10 minutes).

    No erasers this time! Place a chair on a table. Explain that the pupils are to draw round the spaces where the chair is, in order to draw the chair. Demonstrate on an IWB or flipchart with another object, not a chair. Pupils have five minutes to sketch. Tell them to ignore the little voice telling them it's daft – this is the Performance Monster. Ask them to tell it to go away for a while, they're busy!

    Make sure children with visual acuity issues are seated near the object to be drawn. Dyspraxic children may demand an eraser. Explain that no one is allowed an eraser. Mistakes are OK. Repeat with a vase of flowers. Ask the pupils to draw round the objects, drawing the space around the objects rather than the objects themselves. Pupils sign and date the pictures, which may seem odd to them but is part of the process of changing the way they look at things when they draw!

2. Draw your hand, looking at your hand and not the paper, no eraser. Draw your hand in absolute detail (10 minutes). Really look at it. Sign and date the picture.

3. Repeat the same exercise with a trainer shoe or a flower. Look at the object, not your paper. Focus completely. Draw it, no eraser (10 minutes). Sign and date the picture.

4. Upside-down drawing (15 minutes). Use Photocopiable 3A. Tape the sheets in front of them. Make sure no pupil can see the version the right way up. The pupils must draw an outline box on their piece of paper, then copy the drawing, upside down. They sign and date the picture. When they turn the picture the right way up, it usually looks pretty good!

5. Now they draw a side portrait of their classmate again, with absolute focus. Tell them to look at the person more than their paper and to use the eraser very little. They sign and date the picture. What do they notice?

Usually, by the time the pupils draw the side portrait and the trainer shoe, they've begun to look and to draw what they see, not what they think they see. Their first and second drawings of the hand are usually very different, as are their first and second side portraits. Pupils may mention an odd feeling of their brain going 'Thrurrup' as they 'get it'. This is pure learning orientation. Use exercises in Edwards's book. Try it yourself. Be prepared to be amazed at how quickly you learn to draw well.

Workshop 4

Come to the Learning Party (1½ hours)

This session uses Howard Gardner's Eight Intelligences.

● Learning intention

Pupils identify the learning activities they really love and find ways to focus on these in lessons.

● Success criteria

Pupils can:

- discuss Howard Gardner's Eight Intelligences;

- identify their natural talents from these intelligences and one they would like to develop;

- use this information to inform their choice of hobbies and to develop their talent areas;

- use buddy work to develop Learning Muscles in one of the Smart areas.

● Resources

Photocopiable 4A (page 32), one for each pupil

Materials for each area listed in section 1 below, Post-it® notes (optional), pens or pencils

▷ Main activity

1. Organise your classroom into eight areas, each with appropriate items, pictures and examples of the intelligences, plus large flipchart sheets to write on and big pens:

   - books, poems, writing materials for Word Smart;

   - maths games for Number Smart;

   - music/instruments for Music Smart;

   - dance video, Twister game for Body Smart;

   - task that needs organising and doing by a group (such as collating and stapling) for People Smart;

   - plants, a scientific experiment, animals books, gardening tools for Nature Smart;

   - art materials, chess game, digital cameras for Picture Smart;

   - a quiet meditative area with materials for a journal for Self Smart.

2. Put chairs round the edge of the room, as at the start of a party, and ask the children to sit down.

3. Hand out Photocopiable 4A and a pen to each child. Ask them to read through the sheet quietly. Have a teaching assistant or peer buddy to help children with reading difficulties or special needs. For some children you may wish to create a simplified version of the sheet with visuals. Autistic children may need to discuss this sheet before the lesson and think through their choices beforehand in a quiet space. When the children have read their sheet, repeat the instructions on the sheet. Ask the pupils to sit and think about which is their group.

4. Pupils write the group's name on their sheet, then move to their first choice of zone. In the zone, they discuss and note on the flipchart sheet under the heading 'Choice 1' (or on Post-it notes, which they add to the sheet) what they have in common with other people in that zone. Why do they really love that type of being smart?

5. Ask the pupils to return to the edge of the room and look at the sheet again. They are to imagine that the group they chose has had to leave the party. They pick their second choice and go to that group's zone, recording their choice on their sheet. Again, they use flipchart paper to record their ideas, taking a second sheet and heading it 'Choice 2'.

6. The children return to the edge of the room. Explain that the second group has left so now they make their third and final choice. They go to that group and repeat the process.

▷ Plenary

Discuss together what has been learned about their favourite learning areas. Celebrate the differences pupils find within these groups, as well as differences between the groups themselves.

Discuss how pupils can bring 'the stuff they love' to every lesson – and to their lives, via hobbies outside school.

▷ Follow-up activities

Find some way to make a class record of pupils' learning party choices. You could use a wall chart.

Alternatively, each group may celebrate their first-choice option, so the Word Smarts write a poem; the Music Smarts write a jingle or song; the Body Smarts devise a dance routine to be filmed and kept; the Number Smarts invent a maths puzzle; the People Smarts think of ways to organise the groups; the Nature Smarts set up a mini garden in the class and care for it; the Picture Smarts sculpt or make a class mural; the Self Smarts may sit back and reflect on it all and produce independent ways of praising their type of smart!

Pupils will understand that all kinds of smart are equally valid and important. All talents are equally wonderful and everyone has talents and skills. If pupils want to challenge the Performance Monster and develop Learning Muscles in areas they like but lack confidence in, encourage them to buddy up with one of the pupils who is smart in that area and work together on projects.

VAK (1½ hours)

◉ Learning intention

Pupils can use their understanding of their VAK preferences to focus better in lessons.

◉ Success criteria

Pupils can:

- identify which of the three preferences for taking in ideas – visual, aural or kinaesthetic, or a balance of these – they prefer to use in lessons;
- identify which preference is their weak spot and needs focus;
- redesign a lesson plan provided by the teacher to include their way of learning.

◉ Resources

Photocopiable 5A (page 33), one for each pupil, pencils, lesson plan for a literacy or maths lesson in simple language

▷ Introduction

Revise how the pupils have already developed their Learning Muscles. Explain that they are going to think about how they prefer to take in ideas.

▷ Main activity

The pupils work alone, or with assistance where needed, to work through the sheet. They score the sheet in pairs, then group themselves according to their prime preference (if they have two equal preferences, direct them to opt for one). In V, A and K groups, they discuss how they take in ideas and what causes problems in classes. Hand out the lesson plan. Talk the class through it and ask each group to devise ways to add their preference for taking in information to what the teacher does in the lesson, or to activities the pupils will do.

Ask the groups to redesign the lesson, then discuss how to present the ideas to the class in their preferred mode – V, A or K. The groups make presentations. Ask the groups watching the presentation to note how much of the presentation they understood and what caused them problems.

▷ Plenary

Ask the pupils what the major problem for them with the presentations was. How did this affect the listening groups? Could they summarise other groups' ideas, or were they confused?

Discuss and agree on ways in which all three modes can be used in lessons and how pupils can build Learning Muscles. Make sure they understand that the way you teach affects their understanding of what you communicate.

What Shape are You? (1 hour)

○ Learning intention

Pupils further analyse the way they prefer to learn.

○ Success criterion

Pupils can identify one way to increase their Learning Muscles.

○ Resources

Photocopiable 6A (page 34), one section for each pupil; Photocopiable 6B (page 35), two to three for each group; Photocopiable 6C (page 36), one for each pupil; pens or pencils and flipchart paper

Introduction

Discuss what they have already learned about using their heads to learn. They share one way they can develop Learning Muscles, in pairs. Then, at their tables, pick one person from each to feed back to the class. If they have done the drawing exercises in Workshop 3, discuss how to get rid of the Performance Monster as they learn – by telling it to go away for a while as they are busy. Encourage them to remind themselves of their preferred ways to take in information (VAK) and the areas in which they like to work (Gardner's Eight Intelligences).

Main activity

The pupils complete Photocopiable 6A. Explain that it is a fun exercise, not to be taken too seriously. Group them by tables by their first choice. Ask them to draw a line down the centre of a piece of paper, then draw their shape at the top. On one side they should write 'We like' and on the other 'We don't like'. They list what they like / don't like when they are learning. They should consider such aspects as whether they like the same timetable, same activities, or different ones each day; and whether they like to work alone or with others. Let them list what they have in common. Share these as a class.

To extend the lesson, ask each shape group to act out what they'd see as the perfect type of lesson. It could be comedic, as in 'If we squares/circles/triangles/squiggles ruled, this is how we'd run the schools!'

Now ask pupils to move to the table that reflects the shape they disliked most. Let them read what pupils who preferred that shape liked when learning. Ask if there are skills listed that the new group of pupils need to develop. Hand pupils Photocopiable 6B, the answer sheet, and Photocopiable 6C, the activity sheet. Let them discuss both and then complete 6C.

Plenary

Ask pupils to discuss what they've learned about their Learning Muscles from this session. What did the shapes exercise tell them that they already knew? What surprised them? What was the key to learning in the shape they rejected? Did they find everyone who rejected that shape had the same skill or area that they need to develop, or different areas?

Workshop 7 – Introduction

One of the most popular workshops I designed and ran during the Newham transition project was SPIQe. It was welcomed by secondary schools as a way to improve reading in English lessons and by Year 6 teachers as a technique to increase reading comprehension skills and speed.

I developed SPIQe in 1999, whilst working as a Year 6 teacher at Hallfield Junior School, Bayswater, London. Educational psychologist Carol Greenaway asked me to teach the skills good readers use via reciprocal teaching: summarising, predicting, investigating (often called clarifying) and questioning. She called it SPIQ. I tried it out.

I taught six reluctant readers (all tested as level 3) in a small group, using reciprocal-teaching techniques. I listened to the pupils' comments about their learning and the techniques evolved from their examples and achievements. In three months, all were level-4 readers and enjoying reading.

Since then I've refined the lessons and techniques with primary and secondary pupils. It is the pupils who've helped me develop SPIQ into SPIQe (adding 'e' for 'eyes' – visualisation – to include the final skill used by good readers). It was also those pilot group Year 6 pupils who came back to class within a week, stating that they were using SPIQe when they read with younger siblings. Additionally, older brothers/sisters who read to them (as most were pupils for whom English was not their first language), and were studying at college, visited and asked me to teach them how to use SPIQe for their own studies.

This is the introductory lesson. Once pupils are able to SPIQe, they can use the skills in guided reading lessons and cross-curricular reading. When pupils read they SPIQe. It takes three to six months of regular use to be effective, but you'll thank me at SATs time. Some of my project secondary schools used SPIQ (before the addition of 'e') in Year 9 and Year 11 classes, adapting the types of questioning used for these older children.

For SPIQe to work, pupils must continue to use the skills in mixed-ability pairs and in paired reading work. The introductory lesson uses only basic on-the-line questioning (QCA type 2 – answer is directly in the text). Once the skills are established, refine by modelling asking between-the-lines questions (QCA type 3 – inference/deduction) and beyond-the-lines opinion questions when pupils use Q (questioning) in SPIQe lessons.

In the National Strategy Renewed Literacy Framework, the core position paper on reading comprehension discusses reciprocal teaching as the method for enabling pupils to draw meaning from text. The DfES core position paper 'Developing Reading Comprehension' (2006) quotes the SPIQe ideas inherent in the work of the USA National Reading Panel (2000) in the section titled 'Comprehension strategies'. To read it, visit the Standards site: www.standards.dfes.gov.uk/primaryframeworks/literacy/Papers/learningandteaching/reading_comprehension/

SPIQe to Read like a Wizard! (1½ **hours**)

▶ Learning intention

Pupils can read for meaning and enjoyment.

▶ Success criteria

Pupils can:

- explain the five skills a good reader uses;
- demonstrate these skills to another pupil.

▶ Resources

Photocopiable 7A (pages 37–38), or any similar story. Use a simple narrative with lower-level vocabulary, not too long. It must have a cut-off point so you can separate the end, and there should be room in the margin for the pupils to write notes. The end is given out later in the session. If you are using 'The Magic Flower', choose where to remove the end of the story. You could pick before the last two paragraphs, when Albus is returned to his house; or remove only the last paragraph, and ask the class to predict what happened to Felix. Cut off the end (after photocopying) before you hand out the story. You will need to distribute the end separately.

Pencils

Arrange the class in mixed-ability reading pairs. Pupils must be able to decode when they read to access SPIQe skills. Those with high special needs in reading, or new to English as a language, will need picture cards for each element of the story. Use websites to find pictures to illustrate the story.

▷ Introduction

Ask the children: 'Who dislikes reading – hands up. What exactly is it that you dislike?'

Responses will probably be along the lines of: boring books, stories too long, too many words, words too small, not enough pictures.

Then ask: 'Who loses the meaning when they read, has to go back and re-read to get the meaning?' Many hands will go up.

Ask: 'What if I can solve this problem for you in one lesson? Who thinks we can do this?' Note on the board the number of children who think you can or can't solve this in one lesson.

Now introduce SPIQe.

Explain and write on the board the five skills good readers use all the time when they read:

S	= **Summarise**
P	= **Predict**
I	= **Investigate**
Q	= **Question**
e	= **eyes** (visualising what is in the story, making films in their head)

Let the children know that they already use some of these skills.

I = INVESTIGATE

Ask the children what they do when they find a word they can't pronounce or whose meaning they don't understand. Classes always reply by giving the following answers – use a dictionary, ask a friend/ teacher, pronounce it out loud, break it into syllables – and usually add: read before and after the word to get the meaning (the context of the text).

Congratulate them and tick I = Investigate as they already know how to do this.

P = PREDICT

Ask who watched TV or a DVD last night and turned to someone with them and said 'He'll die / They won't get married' or something similar. Congratulate those who put their hands up and say they were predicting.

Ask them to think about these titles: 'Word problems in multiplication' and 'The parts of a plant'. What sort of text would these have written under the titles? Pupils will name the subject areas. Say 'Congratulations: you were predicting.'

Tell them the title of the story you are using and say, for example, 'The Magic Flower – what do you think this story will be about? What will it tell you about?' Pupils discuss this in pairs (1 minute) and then feed back (all pairs).

Say again: 'Congratulations – you were predicting.' Now explain that they will learn about the two other big skills.

Main activity

Hand out the story without the ending – one between two – and give each pair a pencil.

S = SUMMARISE

Tell the children to follow the instructions you will give, with their partner. They should fold over the story so they can just see the first paragraph and do as follows:

1. Read – one reads to the other, aloud, and both look at the story. While doing this, both are thinking 'What is the main thing that is happening in this paragraph?' (Who/What/Where)

2. Natter – they talk to each other and agree the main idea/points.

3. Bullet points – they write the main idea, in note form, beside the relevent paragraph.

   (3 minutes for these three tasks)

The pupils do paragraph 1, and write their bullet points. Stop the group, and encourage them to discuss and agree on the main idea. Often they give too little or too much information on their first attempt. Watch for re-telling the story in different words. If it happens, point out that it is a mistake and explain the difference between paraphrasing and summarising.

Repeat this process for paragraphs 2, 3 and 4. The pupils will speed up as they go. Tell them to fold the paper, showing only the new paragraph and previous paragraphs each time, and do one paragraph at a time as above – read, natter, bullet points, share. Once the children begin to understand S, you can introduce Q. Otherwise keep Q for the next lesson.

Q = QUESTION

Explain that Q and S work together. If you can summarise the main idea of a paragraph, you can ask a question about that paragraph to check that you have got the main idea.

Model this with a previously read paragraph – on-the-line questions only at first. Model good and poor questions. Ask them to develop a question verbally for another paragraph. After 1 minute share the questions quickly and ask a pupil from another pair to answer each question given.

Point out that the ending of the story is missing and explain that you're about to give it to them. First, they should read the notes they wrote down the side of the story. Ask if they can see that the story is summarised there. If they can, they're good summarisation notes. If they can't, something is wrong with their S. Discuss quickly.

P = PREDICT

Before you hand out the ending, ask the pairs of pupils to predict the ending. Share what they say.

Hand out the ending. The pupils read and discuss the actual ending and their predicted ending. Make sure they understand that they are both OK. They are thinking like writers when they predict endings.

e = EYES

Ask the pupils to close their eyes, heads down, and think about what the flower looks like – its shape and its colour. They should put up their hands if they think the magic flower was blue/green/yellow or another colour. Record on the board the number who chose particular shapes, such as daisy or rose. Ask them to open their eyes. Show them the results. Ask them to look at the text. Does it state anywhere what the flower looked like? No. Explain that they were visualising, using their inner reading eyes when they did this. That means they already know this skill also.

You could also ask them to sketch the gigantic flower and the urn that Felix saw. When they compare the pictures they will see how everyone visualises differently.

▷ Plenary

1. Ask the pupils to explain to the person next to them how to summarise.

2. Next, ask them to do a thumbs-up if they could do this. If yes, tick S on the list (SPIQe) on the board.

3. Ask them to explain to you how to I = investigate – tick I on the list again. Do they have an example of a word in the text that they investigated as they read? Share quickly.

4. Ask them to explain to their partner how and why we use Q (if done in lesson) and share. Tick on the board, or note if this needs more work.

5. Ask them to explain to you what e is about. Tick e. Repeat for P.

6. Look at the success criteria. Ask: 'Haven't you just explained this?' Could they go home tonight and demonstrate SPIQe to a parent or younger child? Thumbs up / across / down.

7. Ask pupils which sections need further work. Ask them if they enjoyed the lesson. Did they read for meaning and enjoyment? Did they lose the meaning? Was it fun? Do those who disliked reading still feel the same?

8. Before they leave the room, get them to practise SPIQe with a partner, using their usual reading book. Pupils need to take the skill into their own practice.

▷ Follow-up – SPIQe your socks off!

1. Re-teach SPIQe within a week, using another text.

2. Use SPIQe every time you read in class; use it for guided reading groups. Independent groups can do SPIQe in pairs.

3. Reinforce pupils' ownership of the learning and skills by setting simple SPIQe home-learning comprehension texts. Ask pupils regularly to do S and write 1–3 questions. Work in class with pupils who paraphrase in homework rather than summarising.

4. Use SPIQe to teach on-the-line, between-the-lines and beyond-the-lines questions. For Year 6, find examples in SATs papers to demonstrate the different types of questions.

5. Encourage pupils to use SPIQe to summarise in SATs reading tests, during reading time.

6. Use SPIQe with factual texts – in science, RE, history and geography.

PHOTOCOPIABLE 2A Who Owns your Learning?

	A	B (Tick one box)
1. Who is responsible for your learning?	Your teacher	You
2. When people you know, or your friends, persuade you to do something wrong, who is responsible for you doing the wrong thing?	You	Your friends
3. We have a fixed amount of intelligence. What you're born with is what you've got for life.	I disagree	I agree
4. We can grow smarter. We can continue to learn and grow our intelligence through experiences.	I disagree	I agree
5. You are given two tasks to do. The first task is really easy, it's very simple, like 1 + 1= ?		
For the second task, you can choose one of the following. Which do you choose?		
Task A – another really simple task, which you can't fail to do well.		
Task B – a task you might not complete correctly, but it will be a challenge.	Task A	Task B

PHOTOCOPIABLE 2B   Who Owns your Learning? Answer Sheet

Name:

Class:

	A	B
1. Who is responsible for your learning?	**P** Your teacher	**L** You
2. When people you know, or your friends, persuade you to do something wrong, who is responsible for you doing the wrong thing?	**L** You	**P** Your friends
3. We have a fixed amount of intelligence. What you're born with is what you've got for life.	**L** I disagree	**P** I agree
4. We can grow smarter. We can continue to learn and grow our intelligence through experiences.	**P** I disagree	**L** I agree
5. You are given two tasks to do. Which do you choose?	**P** Task A	**L** Task B

Add up your total score for each.

I have scored: **P** [   ]   **L** [   ]

P = Performance orientation   L = Learning orientation

Which has the highest score (circle)? Performance / Learning

Performance Monsters

- You think your intelligence is fixed, and that this fixed ability leads to your success.

- You want to do well in tests and to seem 'smart' to those around you.

- You like to compete with others and do better than them. You want to prove you're smart to those around you.

- If you fail, you think it's because you're not smart enough, or you're not smart in that type of work.

- You don't like failing, so you won't take risks. Taking risks means that you may fail. You like to avoid risks.

- When a task is difficult, you may act helpless, say 'I can't do it!' and give up.

- Given the choice of trying an adventurous task, one you might not succeed at, or an easy task you can do without failing, you tend to pick the easy task.

- If you do something wrong as a result of listening to others, you tend to blame them, rather than admit you made the choice.

- You may think that you don't control your own life, that your mistakes are the fault of outside situations and other people.

Learning Muscles

- You believe that your intelligence can grow as you learn, that you can always learn more and be more.

- You believe you have the ability to learn and improve.

- You believe that effort leads to success.

- You're willing to make mistakes, to take on challenges, even when you may not succeed. Challenges are good, mistakes are OK.

- You learn from your mistakes, they help you learn. You're not afraid of making mistakes.

- You persist; you like to learn new skills.

- You talk to yourself when you're engaged in tasks.

- You get satisfaction from success as you define it – doing difficult tasks.

P Performance orientation

POSITIVE	NEGATIVE	INTERESTING

L Learning orientation

POSITIVE	NEGATIVE	INTERESTING

Based on the ideas of Edward de Bono.

This workshop is inspired by one in *Drawing on the Right Side of the Brain*, by Betty Edwards.

PHOTOCOPIABLE 4A Come to the Learning Party

1. When you arrive at the party you discover you can be with only one group of children. Whom will you pick? Which group is most like you, and doing the activities you really love? Imagine you join that group because it's your group.

Note their name here: _____

2. Rats! After 15 minutes that group has to leave. You can't go with them. Of the remaining groups, which is most like you now, has activities you enjoy and want to do? Think about it carefully.

Imagine yourself joining that group and note their name here: _____

_____

3. Oh no, it happens again! After 15 minutes they have to leave and you need to pick a third group to talk to and join in. Which remaining group is most like you? Imagine you join that group.

Note their name here: _____

NUMBER SMART – YOU LIKE TO COUNT IT
Like formulae, calculations, logic, maths. Like finding number patterns, sequences, geometry, algebra.
Design mazes or number puzzles.
Like frameworks for thinking and writing. May like to add up prices while shopping, as a game.
Like spidergrams, with neatly ruled lines, rather than picture mind maps.
Enjoy putting ideas in their correct order.
Given an architectural design for a home, want to draw an exact plan for the house.
Interested in designing programs for computers.

WORD SMART – YOU LIKE TO TALK, WRITE, ARGUE
Like to read, write, speak, debate, write fiction or non-fiction.
Enjoy reading dictionaries and thesauruses for the fun of it.
Enjoy taking part in a mock trial for history, being a lawyer for one side.
Like to read and write poems. You love words.
Like to practise jokes to make people laugh, or speak in public.
Remember really good lines from films.

PICTURE SMART – YOU LIKE TO DRAW IT, MAKE IMAGES
Draw, paint, sculpt. You enjoy playing chess and can remember the moves. Can keep chess moves and computer games moves in your head as pictures.
Love creating mind maps.
Can visualise objects from different angles – above, to the side, below.
Find it hard to understand that other children find this difficult.
Like the idea of designing houses, castles, buildings.
Like the visuals on computer games and using graphics packages on PCs.
Like digital cameras.

MUSIC SMART – YOU LIKE TO SING, HUM, MAKE SOUND EFFECTS
Hum and sing to yourself a lot.
Can hear the music in people's voices, that they all sound different.
Can mimic people's voices and accents.
Like to sing or play an instrument. Like to invent your own music.
When walking alone, can sing to yourself, making up tunes or songs.
Remember nursery rhymes or songs you learned when little.
Download music tracks to listen to while on a PC.
Music makes you happy. Can feel the rhythm of music, tap it out. Can rap, though it's the sounds you like rather than the words. Can make sound effects.

BODY SMART – YOU LIKE TO MOVE!
Want to dance, play sports, move, move, move!
Use lots of gestures when you speak; move your hands, arms, face.
Like to act out things in class rather than drawing them.
Like to mime, play games in which you move, good at balancing.
Don't like to sit still, unless watching sports. Even then, would rather play than watch.
Friends know when you're happy, angry or upset – show it with your whole body.
Think of being an actor, dancer, model or sportsperson. When you watch dance tracks on TV, learn moves and can do them and show others.

NATURE SMART – YOU LIKE THE REAL WORLD, INVESTIGATING IT
Street Smart, because you pay attention to the world round you, and Nature Smart – like to be outside, playing, being around plants, animals and the real world. May enjoy preparing and cooking food.
Like to look after animals, grow plants and vegetables in your own garden.
Like the smells and sounds and sights of nature. Don't mind the mess.
Remember how to grow plants and care for animals. Like field trips and camping. Like to be a gardener, hunter, zookeeper, vet, forest ranger or a chef. Good with pets and remember all the things they need to be safe.

PEOPLE SMART – YOU LIKE TO WORK WITH PEOPLE AND GET THE BEST FROM THEM
Like to work in groups and organise others, rather than being alone to study.
Aware of the moods and feelings of other pupils and your teachers.
Enjoy group activities; happiest when you're part of a happy group.
Important for you to help others solve their problems with friends.
Like to be a peer mediator.
Can see how people can work well together in a group.
Quite like to be a teacher or to run your own business when you're older.

SELF SMART – YOU LIKE TO REFLECT ON LIFE, KNOW YOURSELF
This is the group that's just you and you're happy for that to be so!
Like a quiet space to be by yourself: to think, write poems or a journal.
You don't dislike other people, or are moody. You really like being alone.
Like to work independently on projects, rather than with others.
Faith or own ideas are very important to you.
You want answers about God, life and the big stuff.
Think very deeply about everything. May pray or meditate.

PHOTOCOPIABLE 5A VAK

**Read through the following three lists of ideas. Think about how you learn best in class.
Tick if you agree with a statement. At the end, add up your total for each list.**

V= VISUAL = You LOOK to learn

I doodle pictures or shapes while I'm listening in class, but I'll keep looking at whoever is talking, too.
To remember ideas, I need to make notes when teachers speak.
To check the spelling of a word, I have to see it, so I write it down and look to see if it looks right.
I make films in my head and daydream a lot in class.
I use lists, graphs, diagrams, maps and notes to understand ideas.
In tests, or when I need to remember an idea, I can often just 'see' it in my head, as in my exercise book or a reference book.
I look at my teacher and friends when they're sharing ideas with me. It helps me focus.
I read everything, even cereal packets and signs on walls. I can't help it!
I say things like 'I can see that' or 'Picture this' or 'That looks good' when I'm talking to people about ideas.
I like using Post-it notes and digital cameras in lessons.
I turn off the sound when I use a PC. It distracts me from the pictures.
When I get upset at school, I have sore eyes, or I have a headache because my eyes hurt.
I don't like bright neon lights in the classroom. I can feel them flickering and they make my eyes hurt.

Add up your totals. V = [ ]

A = AURAL = You LISTEN to learn

I prefer someone to tell me an idea, rather than make me read it.
I talk to myself a lot and may sing to myself while I work. Sometimes I don't notice I'm doing this.
To work out a spelling, I'll say the word to check it sounds right, then write it out.
When I'm lost in an area, I prefer people to give me instructions. I can remember them.
I don't have to look at teachers when they speak. I'm paying attention, I hear them, but sometimes they think I'm not and ask me to repeat what they said. I can always do that quite easily. It surprises them!
I'm really sensitive to sounds around me in the classroom. Sometimes I lose focus in lessons because I'm listening to birds or leaves in trees, or sirens outside, or a music lesson in another class. I can't help it!
I say things like 'That doesn't sound right to me' or 'I hear what you're saying.'
I call out the answers in class and can talk back. I don't mean to, but the words just pop out!
I download background music on the PC when I'm learning, but sometimes it distracts me. I don't like too much quiet unless I'm trying to concentrate. I like sound effects on the PC, too.
Sometimes, people's voices and accents sound like music to me.

Add up your totals. A = [ ]

K = KINAESTHETIC = You DO to learn

To learn, I need to do things, not sit and listen or look.
I fidget, I play with pencils and rock on my chair. I can learn when I'm fidgeting. It helps me concentrate.
I move around when I read.
I need to learn in real-life situations.
I do dance moves, or practise football techniques under the table in class.
I use my hands when I talk. I watch how the teacher moves. I prefer it if they move rather than standing still.
I like taking stuff apart and putting it back together to see how things work.
I like to make models or sculpt.
To spell a tricky word, I'll write it in the air or sense it moving around. I like the moving shapes in handwriting.
I enjoy learning through use of drama activities, dance or PE or by doing science investigations.
I notice when my clothes are itchy or uncomfortable. I prefer soft clothes and shoes.
I prefer using PCs to play games where you have to move the cursor quickly.
I say things like 'I don't feel good about that' or 'Get a grip' or 'I need to move to do that.'
When I get upset in class, I get a stomach ache or the muscles in my legs or arms hurt.

Add up your totals. K = [ ]

Put VAK in order for you.   1 = [ ]   2 = [ ]   3 = [ ]

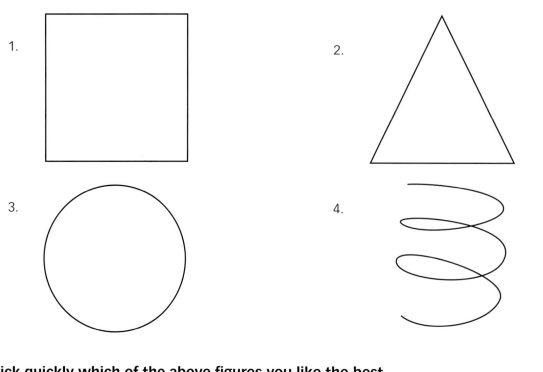

1. **Pick quickly which of the above figures you like the best.**
2. **And the second best?**
3. **Which one do you really dislike?**
Fill in below:

I prefer _____ and then _____ . I really dislike _____ .

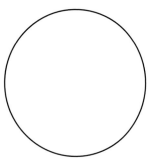

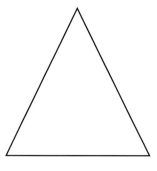

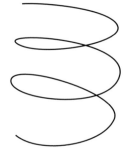

1. **Pick quickly which of the above figures you like the best.**
2. **And the second best?**
3. **Which one do you really dislike?**
Fill in below:

I prefer _____ and then _____ . I really dislike _____ .

PHOTOCOPIABLE 6B What Shape are you when you Learn?

1. Square

* I like specific instructions. I like having the same teacher.

* I prefer a regular timetable during the day. I don't like it when lessons or classroom furniture are changed around. I get upset if there is a supply teacher or if my daily routine is changed. I like to know what is happening and when.

* I like doing what I already know and repeating a technique till I get it right. I am patient and will keep working on a task until I complete it. Sometimes this means I don't like new ways to do things in class, or new methods.

* I don't like risks or making mistakes.

* I am usually very neat and tidy.

If you rejected the square – you don't like routines, regularity and fixed instructions. You like doing things your way!

2. Triangle

* I need to have a goal to work towards. I like achieving steps on the way. I enjoy achieving goals. I like to lead teams. I need a goal and a quest, like a hero on a journey.

* I'm not so good with details. I need squares to help me with them.

* Sometimes, I have so many plans and dreams – all in the future – that I don't get anything done now!

If you rejected the triangle – you don't like to set goals, or work step by step towards goals.

3. Circle

* I need to talk about what I'm learning.

* The most important thing to me is that people get on together and are friends.

* I like to work with others to learn.

* When working in class, I spend too much time ensuring everyone is happy and working together, rather than on the task itself.

* I like colours and plants and music in my learning environment. I want people to feel that the classroom is our home.

If you rejected the circle – you really aren't worried about working with other people or about people getting on with each other to learn.

4. Squiggle

* I need to have lots of new learning experiences. I get bored with the same old routines each day.

* I look at things in an unusual or unexpected way.

* I don't like knowing where the learning will end. Learning is an adventure.

* I'm not patient with step-by-step methods. I have zippy ideas, but sometimes I don't work them through. Instead, I go chasing another new idea.

* Triangles help me plan how to use my ideas. Circles help me work better with others and squares remember the details!

* I don't mind when the timetable changes. I can be really messy! Mess when I'm working or thinking doesn't bother me.

If you rejected the squiggle – you don't like adventures or the unexpected in learning. You prefer safe systems and repeating ideas until you get a safe answer.

PHOTOCOPIABLE 6C Using the Shapes you are to Learn

I prefer the _____ shape (1st choice), because these are the ways I like to learn:

- _____
- _____
- _____
- _____
- _____

I also like to use the ideas of the _____ shape (2nd choice) to learn because I like to:

- _____
- _____
- _____
- _____
- _____

I don't like the ideas of the _____ shape (rejected choice) which are:

- _____
- _____
- _____
- _____

When I think about what I need to change in my learning to grow my Learning Muscles, I find the skills I need to develop from the shape I don't like are:

- _____
- _____
- _____
- _____
- _____

PHOTOCOPIABLE 7A The Magic Flower

Long ago, in a tiny village, there lived a poor boy called Albus, and his mother Maria, who was very ill. His father had died and there was no money for doctors. Albus loved his mother. He remembered her kind voice and her exquisite, sparkling eyes before she became ill and was racked with coughing, sleepless nights and pain.

To help pay for herbal medicines from the local healer, Madame Vita, Albus chopped wood in the forest and carried it to her home. Although it was autumn – cold, windy and wet – Albus worked in her herb garden whenever she asked. The local landlord's son, an evil, lazy boy named Felix, used to tease Albus and laugh as he worked, mud covered, in the garden.

Yet his mother continued to become weaker. Madame Vita took Albus aside and whispered that there was only one thing that would cure Maria. It was the crushed petals of the magic flower. Albus would have to travel through the dark, wintry forest to a garden on the top of a tall mountain, wherein grew the magic flower. If he were worthy, the flower would allow itself to be taken home and would grant him one wish.

Unbeknownst to Albus and Madame Vita, Felix was listening outside the window. He decided that the magic flower should belong to him. It would make him rich! He rushed off, on his horse, thinking he would beat Albus to the prize. Albus had no horse and would have to walk through the forest and up the mountain. He, Felix, had a fine horse and good food, and was noble. He would beat the little peasant to the prize.

Albus took some rough bread, fruit Madame Vita gave him from her garden and a cloak and scarf from his mother and set off, with a strong staff cut from a branch of the oak tree in Madame Vita's garden.

Felix galloped through the forest. Suddenly, his horse reared. An old man was on the path. 'Help me, kind sir, I am so hungry. May I have some food?' he wheezed.

'No, fool! Get out of my way, I'm in a hurry!' screamed Felix, pushing the old man over and galloping away towards the mountain.

When Albus walked through the forest later in the day, he found the old man, leaning against a tree, a gash across his head.

'Help me, kind sir, I am so hungry,' pleaded the old man to Albus.

'I have little, but certainly I will share my bread with you, sir,' replied Albus. He used his mother's scarf to bind the old man's gash and shared the bread with him.

'You've done well, young sir,' smiled the old man. He clapped his hands – once, twice, three times. There was a flash of light. Albus was thrown back to the ground in a faint.

Felix galloped on, spurring on his horse cruelly, up the mountain, to where the garden was. He dismounted, ran into the garden and looked around. Where was this magic flower? He saw a gardener. He was too arrogant to recognise the old man from the path.

'You, gardener, I am a noble boy, here to take the magic flower. Show me it, now!'

The old man quaked in a fluttery voice: 'But, sir, if you are noble you will surely find the flower straight away, without my humble help.'

Felix sneered and clomped off round the garden, destroying plants and kicking trees. He then saw a gigantic, magnificent flower, in an impressive urn.

'Aha!' he yelled, triumphantly. 'I have it!' He ripped out the plant, leaped on his horse and galloped away down the mountain.

The old man then clapped his hands – once, twice, three times – and Albus awoke to find himself inside the garden, at the feet of the old man. He leapt up, apologising for having fallen on a plant.

'Kind sir, where am I?' asked Albus.

'You are in the garden you sought, Albus,' smiled the old man. 'Now, find the magic flower.'

'May I take this flower with me when I find it, sir?' asked Albus.

The old man whispered, 'It has been here awaiting you, Albus. Look around and choose carefully.'

Albus tiptoed round the garden, admiring the trees and plants. He saw a small, young tree, buckling and bent over, needing support to grow straight. Tutting, Albus stuck his staff into the ground by the tree and used the belt from his trousers to straighten it and support it. When he moved the branches, he jumped back in shock.

There, in the shade under the tree, was a tiny flower whose petals were the exact colour of his mother's eyes, sparkling just as hers used to before she became ill. Smiling, Albus knew he'd found the magic flower.

The old man clapped again – once, twice, three times – and Albus found himself home, in his house. Madame Vita was there. She took the flower and held it under his mother's nose. As if by magic, she was instantly healed. Albus hugged his mother and took the flower out to the garden to plant it under a tree.

As for Felix – well, when he galloped back to his grand house and leaped off his horse, with the gigantic flower, to show to all, it suddenly exploded in a puff of the most dreadful stink you can imagine. The horse ran away and Felix's family threw up. No one could go near him as the stink of the exploding flower was all over him. No matter how many times he washed, the stench remained … for all his days … which were pretty lonely ones at that!

4. Listen to your heart workshops

Build bridges instead of walls and you will have a friend.

Anonymous

The most powerful agent of growth and transformation is something more basic than any technique: a change of heart.

John Walwood

Think back to your own move from primary to secondary or middle school. There was a lot of change. Do you remember the academic changes, the changes in friendships, and becoming used to the new, larger environment? Usually, it's the heart (friendship) and gut instinct (being safe and knowing what to do) issues that have stayed with us. The heart workshops in this chapter are the start of the journey for the children you teach. You can amplify and extend them through your PSHE lessons and SEAL activities.

Listening to your heart covers these areas for pupils:

- Being me and being with others.

- Communicating who I am and what I like.

- Making friends and keeping friends.

- Being a good friend.

- Dealing effectively with others who may not be friendly.

These are workshops that touch areas of great sensitivity – both for you, as teachers, and for your pupils. Adapt and change them to the needs of your pupils, but do not pussyfoot. Your 11-year-old pupils are able to deal with emotions at a deep level, in a caring environment, so give them that opportunity. You will be surprised by their honesty and maturity. Help them honour their emotions and grow stronger. With a little more adaptation, you can use them equally effectively for those moving to middle school. They may also be used with Year 7 pupils in secondary school by focusing on their experience of the change to another school, rather than their anticipation of it.

Please note that in these workshops you should give space to children who have been through chaos and difficulty in their lives. Give them options when completing some of the activities. Do not push children to share when they wish to keep pain or emotions private. Ensure that each of these workshops ends with a quiet time in which they can centre and be calm. Always end each workshop by encouraging anyone who wants to talk to you afterwards, or whenever they feel the need to, to do so. Ask your pupils if they have someone they trust to speak to about any emotional issues they have and encourage them to set up this relationship, at home or at school, or in their faith group.

Stepping Stones in Life (1½ hours)

> ❍ Learning intention

Pupils understand that life is a journey, with changes.

> ❍ Success criteria

Pupils can:

- identify the change events in their lives;
- investigate how they've dealt with change;
- discuss the five stages of change, relating them to their life's stepping stones.

> ❍ Resources

Photocopiable 8A (page 57), one for each pupil

Photocopiable 8B (page 58), one for each pupil

CD of quiet classical music to play while Photocopiables 8A and 8B are completed; Photocopiable 8C (page 59); this could be displayed in a prominent place

Pens or pencils; large sheets of cardboard or carpet squares – three for each group of six pupils

▷ Introduction

Discuss how our lives are a journey, as if going down a long, winding road.

Show your own life's journey – your completed journey map – on a flipchart or IWB. Use simple sketches and drawings and quick notes, from start to now, with the five most important events circled.

Give each pupil a copy of Photocopiable 8A. Explain that they will have 20 minutes to think about their lives and to fill in the sheet with drawings and notes to form an autobiography, starting at the top of the page, from when they were born. Discuss and list on the board what they will draw and write about: places where they've lived, moves and their age when they happened, births and deaths among their families and/or friends, important events, holidays, achievements, groups they've joined, pets.

Note that this is a quiet, private task. They will not be asked to share their sheet. Play classical music quietly in the background while they complete it. Ensure that special needs pupils and those who are emotionally vulnerable are given support in this activity. Dyspraxic pupils may need a time line to help them work from being young to their current age. Autistic pupils may not record emotions attached to events, and may organise their life's events in the way that is important to their internal system of understanding the world. The way a pupil chooses to complete this task is up to them.

▷ Main activities

Hand out a copy of Photocopiable 8B to each pupil. Ask the children to refer to the Life's Road worksheet (8A) showing their life and find five major changes in it until now. Those are the changes that are important to them. They should write or draw one change in each of the five shapes, and answer these questions:

- What was the change?

- How did you feel about the change then?

- How do you feel about the change now?

For autistic children, change 'feel' to 'think' and discuss with them what they thought about the fairness of the change.

Now ask pupils to share, in pairs that have been organised with care by you, the what, how then and how now answers for the most important of their changes – or the change they are willing to share with another person.

Discuss the difference between the way pupils felt then and the way they feel now about the change. Perhaps they now accept a change that they found difficult when it happened.

Introduce the Five Phases of Change model shown on Photocopiable 8C to the pupils.

Ask the pupils to look at the example they have just discussed. Are they aware that their feelings have changed? Which of the times seemed the most difficult? Ask them to consider how moving to another school will be a change in their lives. Discuss and write on the board what they're likely to say and do at each phase. Keep the model on flipchart paper for future reference.

Plenary

End the workshop with the Stepping Stones game, played in a hall or outside. If there is a pupil in a wheelchair who is to be involved in this game, their wheelchair becomes one of the squares. Pupils can stand next to the wheelchair and be 'on a square' but they must not pull on the wheelchair, or sit on, pull or push the child in the wheelchair. Check with the pupil that they are OK with this and model for health and safety. Children with sight, hearing or physical disabilities may choose to have a buddy, who can stay with them on their square. Ensure all children can participate.

Each team of six is given three large carpet or card squares. The aim is to move their entire team safely from one side of a crocodile-infested river to the other side. Use chalk or markers to indicate the sides of the river.

All members of the team must fit on one of the squares. If anyone falls off, they aren't eaten by crocodiles – oh, no; instead, the team loses a square. It's a communication, planning and team co-operation game.

When the game has been played, ask your class what its aim was. Once they've given their answers, let them know it was about learning to co-operate and work as a team. Ask teams that completed the task what skills they used and how they worked together. For teams with issues and problems, what went wrong? Pupils should answer without laying any blame on others.

Ask the pupils to sit quietly and think about this workshop. What was the real theme of this game, in terms of their move to a different school? Being able to work with others and befriend people is important in secondary or middle school. Set a quiet thinking time to end the workshop. Explain that future workshops will deal with the issues of being a good friend and making new friends.

Workshop 9

Be a Friend and Find a Friend **(1½ hours)**

○ Learning intention

Pupils can identify what they can offer others as a friend and what they seek in friends.

○ Success criteria

Pupils can:

- discuss their own good points;

- recognise that what they seek in a friend is what they like in themselves and what they dislike in others is what they dislike in themselves (projection).

○ Resources

Photocopiable 9A (page 60), one for each pupil. Prior to the lesson, each child has a photograph taken and printed as a small picture in the centre of the sheet.

Photocopiable 9B (page 61), one for each pupil; pens or pencils

▷ Introduction

You will need to work in a large space for some activities.

Hello game

Everyone stands in their own space. Tell the class to walk around without bumping into anyone. Then give them instructions as follows:

Walk normally. Stop. Walk as if the floor is covered in delicate glass crystals. Stop. Walk normally. Walk as if the floor is covered in thick custard. Stop.
Walk around the room and shake hands, saying 'Hello' to each person you meet, then move on to another person. I will change the emotion you need to feel when you say 'Hello'.
Walk around. Say 'Hello' in a happy voice. [*Give pupils time to move around and experience this.*]
Stop. Walk around, say 'Hello' in a sad voice. What do you notice your body does? Your voice? [*Give pupils time.*]
Stop. Now, walk and say 'Hello' in an angry voice. Notice your voice, your body, how the other person reacts to you, how you feel.
[*Repeat with other emotions: upset, scared, impatient, uninterested.*] **Stop.**

Ask everyone to sit on the floor in groups of 4. Encourage them to discuss what they noticed about their voices, feelings and body (how they held themselves when using different emotions). Get them to think about how a simple 'Hello' said in a negative emotion can affect their day.

▷ Emotions in your body game

The pupils stand and find their own space. Ask them to recall how they used the emotion changes in the first game. Explain that now you're going to take time and, standing in one place, gradually build an emotion from 0 (no emotion) up to 10, with the emotion at full power, then go back to 0. You will tell them the emotion and count from 0 to 10, hold, then back to 0. Tell the pupils they need to think of a time when they experienced the particular emotion, then imagine being in that state again. They have to fill themselves up with the emotion. At the end of each 0 to 10, 10 to 0, ask them to shake off the emotion and breathe deeply in and out.

Use the following emotions: sad, then angry, then happy.

Sitting on the floor, the pupils discuss in pairs what they noticed about where in the body the feelings of anger, being upset and happiness seem to live and how their bodies changed. Encourage them to share the ideas. Discuss how this information is useful. You need to bring out that it helps us 'read' body language when people are getting angry or upset and to give them time to calm down. Ask the children to stand, feel really miserable and sad, then to look up at the ceiling, put an enormous smile on their faces and yell 'Yes, yes'. Ask what happens. They should say that the sadness vanishes. Explain that this demonstrates how emotions can be changed when you change your body movements. Obviously this is not a solution to deep emotional issues, but a good way to make a fast change when you're feeling cranky.

Talk about why exercise is effective for them: it releases endorphins and makes them feel good. Ask them to think about how they feel if they've sat in front of a television for days and days over a holiday, and how their feelings changed when they played outside.

▷ Main activities

Be a friend and find a friend shopping list

1. Give each pupil their copy of Photocopiable 9A, with their own photograph in a small box in the centre. Round the page they are to mind map what makes them a good friend: what they like, the good things about them as a person. They should try to identify five to seven things. Give them time to do this alone. Special needs pupils should be given help by a teaching assistant, the teacher or a buddy.

2. Give each pupil Photocopiable 9B. Model the exercise, working with a pupil or adult who has been briefed about how to do this activity.

- The partner asks you 'What do you really value in a friend?' and lists your ideas in the top section of the sheet. When you stop, they say 'And what else would you like in a friend?' Answers must be expressed as positive qualities (not, for example, 'Not mean, but 'Generous'). Each time you run out of ideas, the partner asks 'And what else?' until you have five to seven attributes listed.

- Then your partner shows you the list and asks you to list them in your order of preference. They write this list in the bottom section of the sheet.

- Now comes the interesting part of the process. You face your partner, seated. Your partner says, 'I've found you the perfect friend. They are …' and lists your preferences, but from the last to the first. Ask the class to watch what happens to your body. There won't be a change. Now, your partner says, 'I've found you another friend. They are …' and lists your preferences from first to last. What happens, involuntarily, is that when that person gets to the second or third item, you will smile and your body will 'puff up' in happiness. Ask the children to note what they saw you do. The point at which you have that reaction is the value that's most important in friendship for you.

- Pupils now follow the same process in pairs, each interviewing the other in turn.

  – What do you value in a friend … and what else … and what else (5–7 items)?

  – Help your partner prioritise their list. Write it on the bottom of Photocopiable 9B.

  – 'I have a friend for you. That person is … [reverse order of values].'

  – 'I have another friend for you. That person is … [correct order of values].' The partner watches for bodily change and notes that against the value that has this effect.

  – Swap and repeat for the other person.

Plenary

Lead a class discussion on the following:

What one thing are you doing now that makes you a good friend? What one thing do you really need to work on in your friendships? Pupils think, then feed back as a group.

- Consider your be-a-friend list and your find-a-friend values. Were they the same or different?

- Did anyone notice that something you know you need to work on is a value you really seek from a friend? Think of something you really dislike in other people. Can you think of times when you've been like this? This is called 'projection'. When we really dislike or really like another person, often we're projecting bits of ourselves that we don't recognise. Do you agree or disagree with this?

- What have you learned today about the types of friends you want to make at your new school?

Have a quiet time during which children reflect on the lesson. You may wish to use a centring exercise to end. Pupils sit comfortably and place their hands on their diaphragms, fingers touching, tip to tip. They breathe in deeply, so that their stomach moves out (shoulders not moving upwards) and the fingertips part. Breathe out, fingers back together. They continue this slow, deep breathing for a few minutes, thinking about the lesson and the ideas they have shared and learned about themselves.

Win–Win Friendships (1½ hours)

▶ Learning intention

Pupils can understand win–win, win–lose and lose–win communication strategies and the way they affect friendships.

▶ Success criteria

Pupils can:

- identify assertive (win–win), aggressive (win–lose) and passive (lose–win) behaviour patterns in themselves and others;
- practise strategies to develop win–win communication and to be aware of and deal with win–lose and lose–win behaviours;
- analyse when they use these behaviours themselves.

▶ Resources

Make cards for Sounds game, one for each group. Write down an event on each card: e.g. You go to the cinema; You attend a birthday party for a younger child; You play a football game; It snows and you make a snowman with your friends; You are on a school trip to a museum where you must be quiet, but your group can't do this; You're having lunch in the hall when a bee flies round your table, trying to get to your cake.

Clipboard, pen and paper for game observers

Photocopiable 10A (page 62), one for each group; cards made from Photocopiable 10B (page 63), to be given out to groups of 3; cards made from Photocopiable 10C (page 64), for trio groups activity

A broadsheet newspaper, sticky tape, scissors, a jug of water and an empty foam cup for each group of six children

▶ Introduction

Sounds game

1. Divide pupils into groups of 5–6. Give each group one of the sound cards you have made. Five (or four) are to play the game; one is to observe the behaviours in the game.

2. Take the observers aside before the game starts and give them each a copy of Photocopiable 10A. Explain that you want them to note when people in the team co-operate and when they don't. Ask them to find an example of co-operation (list it under Assertive); of bossy behaviour (list under Aggressive); and of when someone becomes uninterested because they feel left out (list under Passive). Observers do not do the activity or show their sheets to the participants.

3. Explain that each group must use the activity on their card to write a short story of about five sentences with lots of sounds. To present the story to the class, in 15 minutes, one person must read the story while the other four make the sounds and act them out as a group, working together.

4. Groups write their short story and rehearse.

5. Groups present their story. Observers continue to note behaviours.

Workshop 10

 ## Main activities

Introduce win–win thinking

Tell the pupils that the game wasn't about sounds at all, but about the way you treat each other when you work together. Explain the following ideas.

Aggressive behaviour – I win, you lose, because I'll boss you around and yell to get my way. Ask the observers for examples of this behaviour – to be given without names of people attached. Ask your students to think of times when they've acted aggressively so it was a win–lose situation. Was it a good idea in the long run? What type of person were they being? How did it feel later?

Passive behaviour – I lose, you win. I don't want to do what you ask, but I agree to do it. I am still not interested, so I do it and am really angry with you, but I don't tell you, or worse, I'm passive/aggressive and somehow manage to sabotage your actions by 'accident', so we both lose!

Again, ask the observers for examples of passive and passive/aggressive behaviour, without naming who acted in this way. Ask pupils to give examples from their own lives of when they've been passive or passive/aggressive. How did it feel?

Assertive behaviour – I win, you win. I say what I think and feel. I won't let you bully me. If you don't want to do something, I'll ask why and I'll accept your views. I accept that we need to reach agreement on issues and work together. Observers give examples of assertive behaviour. Pupils are asked to think of a time when they've co-operated, or when they've told a friend they were hurt and have sorted out a problem. How did it feel? How does it feel compared to being aggressive or passive?

Practising win–win

Now suggest they practise becoming more assertive, with some simple techniques. Point out that in situations of danger, they need to be careful – to run away if possible, if it's a mugging, or hand over their stuff and don't argue. The assertiveness technique is for dealing with aggressive and passive behaviour by your friends and people you meet in everyday life.

Also explain that when people are very upset, they need time to express the emotion before they can listen to you. Model giving the other person time to be angry before you speak to them.

Add that the key to win–win communication is active listening, and that they must focus on each other. The assertive person is trying to find a solution in which both sides win.

Place pupils in trios. Hand out cards made from Photocopiable 10B.

Give one aggressive and one passive card made from Photocopiable 10C to each trio.

With volunteers, model one of these scenarios, then ask the trios to practise their scenarios, with two playing the roles and one as a helpful observer.

Plenary (30 minutes)

Review and newspaper tower game

A pair of pupils act out an aggressive scene, then another pair act out a passive behaviour scene with their assertive techniques. The class help with positive feedback. Model how you want feedback phrased: 'I think you did x very well. You could also have done y' rather than 'That was silly. You should have done this.'

Summarise, explaining that these skills take lots of practice.

End the workshop with the newspaper tower game. Now your class is aware of passive, aggressive and assertive behaviours, get them to work again in the same teams as at the start of the session – observers now join in as well – to complete a challenge in 10 minutes.

Give each group of 5 or 6, at a table, a broadsheet newspaper, a jug of water, scissors, sticky tape and an empty foam cup. (The foam cup is provided in case a wily group realise that they can put water in the cup and use that to produce a mushy paper base for their tower. Don't tell them!)

Tell the groups that they have 10 minutes to build the tallest newspaper tower on their table with the resources provided. Remind them that active listening and co-operation will lead to the best result.

The winning group is the one with the tallest tower.

Share and discuss how they worked together. Were they aware of aggressive and passive behaviours and did they help each other to achieve the task as a team? End with a quiet thinking time.

Workshop 11

Money Shapes Game (1½ hours)

◗ Learning intention

Pupils can answer the question 'Which is better – co-operation or competition?'

◗ Success criteria

Pupils:

- begin to combine everything they've learnt in the workshops within a task: i.e. they use their preferred method for taking in information (VAK) on the stuff they like to do (Gardner's Eight Intelligences), working the way they prefer (Shapes);

- develop Learning Muscles by facing the challenge of the Money Shapes game;

- use assertive listening and win–win strategies to work as teams.

◗ Resources

Large quantity of 2D plastic or wooden shapes: triangle, circle, rectangle and square. These should be of similar dimensions.

Scissors (at least 20 pairs), pens (at least 20)

A4 paper, preferably in a colour not usually used in the class

Money – large quantity of yurgles currency made from Photocopiable 11A (page 65)

Bag for each team for rubbish, tray (or bag) for shapes sales

Stickers for each team: Buyer, Seller, Managing Director, Production Manager, Cleaner, Cutter; plus spare stickers for other roles

Rubbish bin by the bank area (to dump sold shapes); flipchart or board

Stickers with red x – for sickness, which you may use to reduce a team's members temporarily

Cards for names of machines

Bell or alarm to signal the start and end of buying/selling rounds

Cards made from Photocopiable 11B (page 66)

Company of the Day Award (made on PC)

▷ Introduction

This session enables the pupils to combine much of what they've learned and practise team building and active listening. They warm up with two fast games, then play the Money Shapes game.

1. Are you listening to me?

Pupils in pairs. One spends exactly 2 minutes telling the other about a favourite holiday or game. The second person then repeats the information back, as if they were the first person themselves – not 'You like …' but 'I like …'. Change places and repeat. Have a quick sharing of what worked in listening actively and what was difficult. Point out that this skill will be vital in the main game.

2. Parts of the whole

Group the pupils into their money game teams of 6 children. Get them to imagine that they will become parts of a working machine. They must practise being the machine. Examples are: tractor, clock, computer, stove with meal being cooked on and in it. Give each team a card with the name of their machine written on it. They have 5 minutes to prepare, 5 to rehearse, and then 2 minutes to present their machine. The rest of the class tries to deduce what machine they are.

Discuss how they planned and worked together. Note that for the Money Shapes game they will need people skills and respect for each other's skills.

▷ Main activity

Explain and set up the Money Shapes game. Ensure that all pupils have an active role and that special needs pupils are included within the teams (or they could assist you at the buy/sell desk). Play the game through at least one round, preferably two, imposing the fines near the end of the first round. The aim is to enable pupils to improve their safety, workspace and team spirit.

Money Shapes game

1. Form teams of 6, each at a large table/tables. Each team is given a bag (for rubbish), Y20 in cash, a tray or bag for the shapes they make and stickers showing their role (see page 48). The Buyer and Seller stickers must be worn at all times. Teams select who will have each role and choose a name for their company.

2. Set up a buy/sell table with: trays of triangle, circle, square, rectangle plastic/wooden shapes, scissors, A4 paper, rubbish bin, pens, large quantity of yurgles currency (in separate sections of a tray). Also set up a large flipchart or board on which to write the price of items.

3. Although you may have assistants, they are not permitted to check the shapes when they are sold, but can sell paper, pens, scissors and shapes.

4. Explain to the class that each team is a company. The task for each company will be to make as much money (yurgles) as possible during the time the game runs. They will be making shapes cut out of paper – and they must buy every item needed to make those shapes from you as the bank.

5. Put up the selling prices: it is Y1 for each shape, sheet of paper, pen and pair of scissors. These may be purchased only by the buyer in each team during the buying period, which will be indicated by you with a bell at the start and finish.

6. When the shapes are made and cut out, they can be brought to you in the market-place to sell by the seller in each team, only when it is a selling time – again to be indicated by you with a bell at the start and end. Teams will not be able to buy and sell at the same time.

7. Warn them that prices for your production materials and for the goods you sell may change during the game. There may be other charges that will be revealed in future rounds of the game. Also warn companies that only the best-quality shapes will be purchased.

8. Teams plan their roles and strategy, and determine what will be purchased. You ring the bell to start and end the buying period. They have about 3 minutes to buy items listed.

9. While they start manufacture, put up the 'selling to you' prices – Y1 for each paper shape.

10. Give teams about 8 minutes to manufacture, then open the selling period. The seller from each table brings their shapes to you to buy. If a shape isn't perfect, refuse it. If it is, buy it, paying Y1 per shape. Tear up the shapes you buy to prevent teams stealing shapes to resell. End the selling period.

11. Have a second buying period. After the buying period has ended change the price of triangles to Y2. Pupils are learning that a market can change unexpectedly.

12. Teams then stop, check their assets and discuss what they've learned so far about running a business and working together. Give teams the option of changing some of the roles in their organisation. Have extra role stickers for this eventuality.

13. Prior to starting round 2, warn the teams that business may change. Fines and fees may be charged. Start the second round with buying. Once buying is ended, put up new prices – Y0 for triangles (glut in the market), Y2 for circles and Y1 for squares and rectangles.

14. As the teams make the shapes, tour the room and begin to charge fees and fines. See Photocopiable 11B for fines or fees. You may also issue rewards for commendations, also on Photocopiable 11B.

15. Hold a selling period. Then hold a buying period, then again change the prices – e.g. glut in circles, so Y0; but shortage of triangles and rectangles, so Y3; Y1 still for squares.

16. At the end of the third selling period, teams check their money. End the game or play another round.

17. At the end of the game, ask the pupils what they learned about running a company and about working with each other. What happened when they became annoyed with each other? Who had to use skills that are difficult for them – e.g. a less confident person as buyer, an impatient pupil as cutter?

18. You may wish to present the Company of the Day Award (made on a PC). Ask the pupils: 'Who wins? The team that made the most yurgles, or the team that worked best together? Was that the same team? What would happen if your company just focused on earning yurgles?' Discuss.

▷ Plenary

Ask the pupils to think back about the game and consider these questions:

1. How did they develop Learning Muscles and face Performance Monsters?

2. Get them to think about their Come to the Learning Party results – the stuff they like to do. How did this game suit each preference? If you are Self Smart, what was it like? What about People Smart? Did you lead, or help people work together? For Music Smart people, was it fun or dull? For Body Smart people, what would working in a factory all day be like?

3. Did the game suit one way of taking in information better than others, or combine each of VAK?

4. In terms of what shape you are when you learn, what did squiggle shape people think of the game? Did triangles run the teams? Did squares do all the detailed work? Were circles making sure everyone got on together? What did you notice?

5. When the rules changed and fines were made, did you become aggressive or passive in your behaviour?

Let's Talk Together (1 hour)

This workshop refers specifically to transition to secondary school, but can easily be adapted to middle school. The planet could be named Midol.

❍ Learning intention

Pupils develop teamwork and communications skills.

❍ Success criteria

Pupils can:

- make a whole-team decision, agreed by all;
- use active listening and assertive techniques within the team task;
- discuss communication issues and how they solved them.

❍ Resources

Photocopiable 12A (page 67), one copy for each pupil

Whiteboards, paper for notes and an A3 or larger-sized sheet for each group to return their verdict. Give teams the option of presenting the verdict in their own way – by oral or kinaesthetic means.

▷ Introduction

Discuss the skills the pupils have already developed and note the issues they had working on the newspaper tower, sounds scene and Money Shapes game. Explain that this workshop is about increasing and improving their communication skills. Ask for suggestions of rules for teams when they work together. Help the pupils to come up with a list that covers the following points:

- Everyone has an equal voice and everyone has a chance to speak and be heard.
- Each team has a leader, and the leader's role is to facilitate (encourage and organise) discussion, not to tell the team a decision or what to do.
- Everyone has to agree to the decision made by the team.
- Set roles within the team: leader, observer, recorder of ideas, assertiveness coach and timekeeper.

Warm-up game

Sit in table teams. Explain that they are to tell a story round the table. Each person says two sentences. The person next to them has to continue the story. Try to do this quickly. Repeat. Ensure special needs pupils and those with hearing difficulties have assistance.

▷ Main activity
Let's Talk Together game

Set the pupils the task on Photocopiable 12A, allowing time to discuss and make a decision (20 minutes).

Remind them that the decision must be unanimous.

You may prefer to use an activity like the dogs' home task from *Thinking Together* by Lyn Dawes, Neil Mercer and Rupert Wegerif.

▷ Plenary

Each team presents their decision and explains how they came to it. Discuss how pupils worked together. What went well? What caused problems? What have they learned about how they will work in groups in secondary school, when they will be with students they do not know well?

Have any of your pupils realised that the eight potential explorers each represent one of Howard Gardner's Eight Intelligences, which they explored in the learning party workshop? Were there intelligences they thought a new planet didn't need? How much were they influenced by the people who would be left behind by the explorers?

Also ask your class what this new planet Secon is. It's the author's little joke about moving to the new planet that is secondary school!

Workshop 13 Introduction to Philosophy for Children

Whilst working as transition consultant in Newham, I supported the introduction of Philosophy for Children (P4C) into my project schools, with training at level 1, P4C.

When practised regularly with a class, P4C is a powerful technique that enables pupils to develop emotional intelligence inside and outside the classroom. It is especially empowering for disaffected pupils, who find the sessions a place to argue constructively and gain respect from classmates for their verbal skills. They also listen assertively to others. Out in the playground they use their P4C skills. Rather than yelling or fighting, these pupils listen and talk to one another to solve issues.

I have also used P4C with Year 6 classes in which pupils have difficulty with metacognition – thinking about their thinking. In Harrington Hill Primary, in Hackney, London, the Year 6 teacher noted that after only two P4C sessions the class began to think more deeply in maths and science lessons. P4C enables pupils to problem solve well, to talk about what they are thinking and to question their ideas.

Students enjoy P4C. In the sessions the teacher is the facilitator. You do not contribute your own ideas at all. What matters is your pupils' ideas and thinking. The moment a teacher says 'I think that …', the P4C session is dead. It takes a lot of patience on the teacher's part to zip their lips and let the children run the discussion. The rewards are improved questioning and thinking skills.

P4C is not circle time, or an ordinary lesson. It does not have to have a lesson plan, learning intention or success criteria. Your major work as a teacher is finding stimuli to begin the lesson, and teaching children the difference between philosophical questions and ordinary questions.

Within the P4C session, you run the order of the activities and facilitate the discussion by indicating who speaks next, though experienced P4C classes know how to run the discussion themselves and give space to one another.

The following workshop is an introductory lesson. You are recommended to contact Sapere (www.sapere.net) to obtain information about P4C training and conferences.

Workshop 13

Introduction to Philosophy for Children (1½ hours)

◐ Learning intention

Pupils can apply speaking and listening skills, and improved emotional intelligence, to philosophical questions.

◐ Success criteria

Pupils can:

- ask philosophical questions;
- listen to classmates' ideas and build on them, agreeing and disagreeing with justification (reasons).

◐ Resources

One of the following: story or poem, picture or image, object or objects, piece of music

For transition you could use a set of images – a slide show of baby; infant; child in nursery, infant school and junior school; then secondary pupil. Or try a short story about transition – 'The Long Walk' by George Layton, or picture books such as *Lost and Found*, Oliver Jeffers, *Cat and Fish*, Joan Grant and Neil Curtis (friendship); *Something Else*, Kathryn Cave and Chris Riddell (being different); *Oh, The Places You'll Go!* (moving on) and *Oh, The Thinks You Can Think!* Dr Seuss (thinking about thinking).

A4 paper for pairs, pen/pencil each

▷ Introduction

Organise the class into a circle of chairs. Initially seat the pupils as appropriate for discussion.

Explain that you will be running a philosophy lesson – P4C – and that it is not circle time, although it may appear to be similar as they are seated in a circle. Philosophy is concerned with thinking and talking about thinking.

Start with a speaking and listening game like Unconnected Words. Child A says a word, such as 'Cabbage'. The next person in the circle has to say a word with no connection to it. If someone else in the circle can think of a connection, they call out 'Challenge'. You select them, and they state the link. If accepted, the next person has to continue from the word before the last word, or choose another word if they're beginning the game anew. You must keep listening! Similar speaking and listening games can be found in *Games For Thinking*, by Robert Fisher. This is a great introduction to listening and challenging ideas.

Stimulus

Read a picture book (or part of a story), showing illustrations to the class, or display a visual image or object, or play a piece of music.

Ask the class to close their eyes and think about the ideas and questions it makes them ask. They do this for 2 minutes.

Asking the questions

Ask your class to open their eyes and to take a piece of paper between two and a pen or pencil each. They should now share their ideas about the stimulus and think about a question they'd like to ask about it.

As they think about questions, ask them to move from questions about the stimulus to a question that is about the ideas or feelings it brings up in them. Explain that if we'd used 'Three Little Pigs', an ordinary question might be 'Why do the pigs build their homes from poor materials?' A philosophical question might be 'Why do we need homes?' or 'What is a home?' Teaching pupils to set philosophical questions is the most difficult part of P4C. Use the guide to ordinary and philosophical questions in *Creating Enquiring Minds* by Sara Stanley. I laminated her sentence starters and gave them to pupils in initial P4C sessions until they were used to the process and ways of thinking and speaking.

Pupils discuss and agree on one question per pair, writing it in large letters on their sheet, with their names underneath.

Sorting the questions

You sit on the floor in the centre of the group. Pupils place their questions on the floor. You then read the questions aloud and ask the class if they can see links between questions. If so, would they like to put two linked questions together? If pupils make this choice, put the two relevant questions side by side.

Voting on the question

The pupils are to pick one question to discuss as a group. You read all the questions aloud once, then each again in the same order. As you read a question the second time, if pupils wish to vote for it they put their pencil on the question. You make a note of the total number of pencils on a question, stop, write that number on the question, then read the next question. Once a question has been selected, you sit back in the circle, holding that question up to the class.

Discussion

Invite the pair of pupils who wrote the question to say, in turn, why they picked that question and share their initial thoughts about it. Open up the discussion to the class. Pupils indicate they wish to speak by putting their hands out in front of them. It isn't a 'hands-up' session. Use sentence starter framers to help students. Remember to make no comment yourself. Pupils are reminded at the start that they are agreeing or disagreeing with other people's ideas. They may start comments with 'I agree/disagree … with … who said … because [give a reason].'

In one P4C session, a pupil with special learning needs asked what one of the words in the question meant. I thanked him as he'd reminded me that we often need to define words in the question. He triggered discussion about definitions of the word in that session and took part confidently in subsequent sessions. His teacher was very surprised as it was unusual for him to ask for help without losing his temper. P4C calmed him and gave him a place to speak and authority within his class.

As facilitator, you may draw out ideas from pupils and ask for reasons for their comments. You may need to restate the question to remind pupils of the P4C theme. This is done in the following way: 'Has anyone else something to add on the question [state the question]?' and wait. Do not ask pupils to speak by name. A P4C session has its own pace and timing. Respect silence and thinking time.

Final round

When I run P4C sessions I have a final round in which a Lion King Trickster® toy is passed round the circle. Every pupil makes a final comment about the question. Pupils who didn't speak up in the initial P4C lesson make one comment here, even if merely to say 'I agree with the question.' I then ask 'What do you agree with?' so they add a few words. As each pupil makes a comment, I thank them.

At this point, pupils often suggest new arguments. The first time this happened, I asked the pupil why he hadn't mentioned this idea in the P4C session. His reply was that it was such a different concept and everyone appeared to be focusing on another point of view altogether, so he wasn't sure whether he should share it. I replied, quietly, that every idea is wanted in a P4C discussion. In the next session this boy began to take part and became an energetic speaker. This was a pupil with poor focus who found it difficult to remain in the classroom for an entire lesson. He would usually just get up and walk out. He stayed in P4C sessions and became a vigorous debater.

By asking reluctant and shy children to make a comment, however small, in the final round, you validate their ideas. They join in more during subsequent sessions. P4C respects all ideas. Pupils recognise that their comments are equally important and valid. I have found teachers to be amazed by the comments children offer in P4C sessions. There is something inclusive about P4C that reaches all pupils.

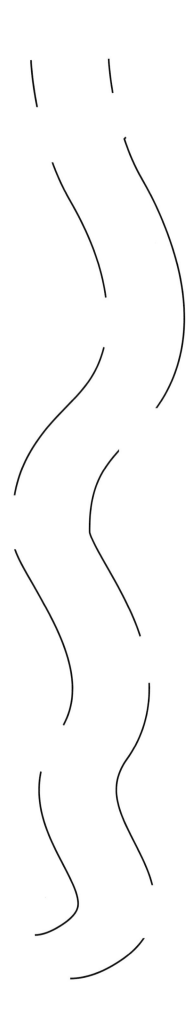

PHOTOCOPIABLE 8C   The Five Phases of Change

The change happens and your emotional response is …

DENIAL

It's not really happening. I got it wrong. I heard wrong. No, there won't really be a change.

ANGER

How dare this happen! It's not fair, I'm furious. How could they do this?

BARGAINING

Hey, I can get rid of this change. If I do X or Y, or promise I'll never do this or that again, well, it'll go back to the way it was, right?

DEPRESSION

What's the point? It's all for nothing. I can't do anything. Life is awful. Everything is dreadful.

ACCEPTANCE

I have to admit it, the change has happened. There's nothing I can do to go back, so let's accept it and move onwards.

This worksheet is based on *On Death and Dying* by Elisabeth Kübler-Ross.

Although designed as a model for grief, it is also a change model.

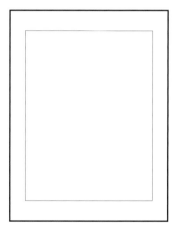

Aggressive behaviour example

Passive behaviour example

Assertive behaviour example

PHOTOCOPIABLE 10B Assertiveness Scripts

Body language and how you speak

When you deal with aggressive or passive behaviour, stand or sit up straight. Look at the person. Speak slowly and quietly. Do not be aggressive or look down, mumbling. Be strong.

When we communicate with others:
- 7% of the message they get is from our actual words;
- 55% is from our body language;
- 38% is from our tone of voice.

Choose your words well and back them up with a positive vocal tone and body language.

Accept the criticism or part of it

'You're always grumpy in the morning.'

Assertive reply: 'You're right. I am grumpy in the morning. I'm trying to improve that by getting more sleep.'
Or part of it: 'Yes, you're right. Sometimes I am grumpy in the morning.'

Disagree with the criticism, using fogging (appearing to agree)

'You always talk about me behind my back!'

Assertive reply: 'You may think that, but I don't talk about you behind your back.'

'You're really lazy.'

Assertive reply: 'You may be right, but I work as hard as I can.'

Disagree, politely, referring to behaviour and giving an example

'You'll never get that story finished. You can't write!'

Assertive reply: 'I disagree. I have written half the story and I will complete it tonight.'

'You reckon! You're a lousy writer.'

Assertive reply: 'I can't agree with that. [*Give behaviour example*.] I had an article in the school newspaper.'

Show you're upset by the comment, but remain calm and disagree

Use 'I', not 'you'.

'Where did you get that jacket? It is ugly, it makes you look so fat!'

Assertive reply: 'I really find that comment upsetting. I like this jacket and I enjoy wearing it.'

'Yeah, and your haircut is really lousy!'

Assertive reply: 'I don't accept your comment. I like my hair, thank you.'

Describe what you don't like and ask for change

'Talk to the hand, I'm not listening.'

Assertive reply: 'When you speak to me so rudely, I'm hurt.'
Additional reply: Say what you want to have happen and what you will do:

'Please look at me when you speak to me. I would like to talk to you but If you cannot be polite, then I will not speak to you.'

Give a person who is angry or upset space to speak

'Jan told me you were talking about me behind my back. How dare you speak about me like that?'

Assertive reply: 'I can see you're really upset. Tell me what's wrong.' [*Listen while your friend gets rid of all their anger, then discuss the problem. Let them get out the anger first.*]

When to walk/run away or get help

If you find yourself facing someone who is very angry, bullying or likely to become violent, get away. You don't have to speak to them. Find an adult, be safe.

If, instead, a friend is very upset and you're worried about them being safe, stay, sit and let them talk. Don't suggest ways to fix things, just listen and offer your help. Get help if it's needed.

PHOTOCOPIABLE 10C   Win–Win Thinking

Passive behaviour scenarios

You've lent your favourite book to a friend and they're giving pitiful excuses for not bringing it back to school. How do you get it back?	You arrange to meet a friend after school to buy a present for your gran. This friend knows exactly where to buy the present but is really reluctant about going with you. They agree to come, then don't turn up. You can't find the shop so you can't get the present. How do you explain to this friend how you feel about what they did?
You want to buy a new pair of expensive, hard-to-find trainers you've seen in a store. You tell a friend who has the same shoe size, then you discover that they have gone to the store and bought the last pair. You can't get them now. How do you feel about their behaviour? How do you tell them and save the friendship?	You have a homework project to complete today with a friend. Your friend comes to your house and keeps mucking around. They want to watch television, play computer games, anything but do the project. You want to do well in this project and you have to complete it together, today. How do you get your friend to work with you?

Aggressive scenarios

A friend wants to copy your homework and is being demanding and rude. They've been too lazy to do it themselves and this isn't the first time they've tried to copy your work.	Someone in Year 7 whom you don't know well demands that you hide a knife in your school bag for them.
A friend borrowed a computer game and won't return it. They tell you they want to keep it. What are you going to do about it?	You drop a £5 note, your friend picks it up and won't return it. 'Finders keepers' is what they tell you.
An adult is really angry with you after you kicked a ball through a window. You know you were wrong. How do you deal with what you did and speak to the adult?	You're playing a game and you're accused of cheating by someone on the winning side, who is very angry. You didn't cheat. How will you deal with this?
Two Year 7 pupils aggressively demand you give them your mobile telephone number. You know they send obscene and bullying messages to people. How do you deal with them?	You take your iPod© to school and a Year 7 pupil tries to snatch it, thinking it's hers. She's not trying to steal it – she doesn't realise her iPod is in the bottom of her bag. She's really popular with the other students and you'd like to be her friend. How do you explain to her that it is your iPod and diffuse her anger?

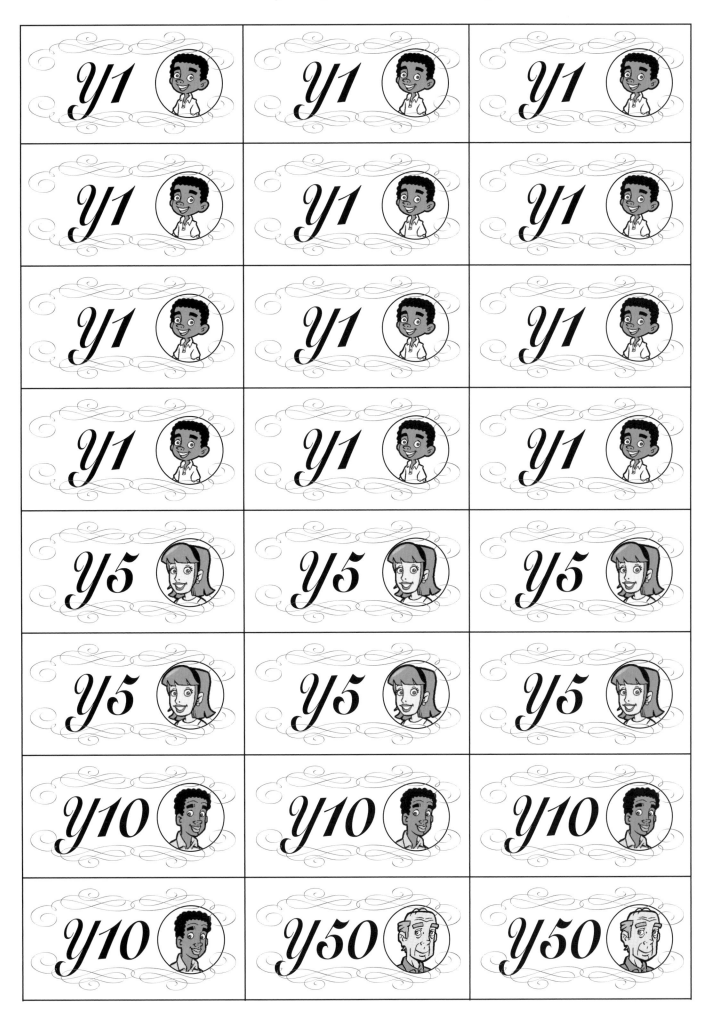

Recycling alert fine

Paper wasted – poor quality goods and cutting

You have violated the Recycling Code by wasting paper.

Pay the bank Y10

Safety alert fine

Scissors managed unsafely

Your company is using unsafe manufacturing techniques.

Pay the bank Y10

Environment pollution fine

Messy table

Your company is damaging the environment by its working practices.

Pay the bank Y10

Noise pollution fine

Noisy teamwork

Your factory is too noisy.

Pay the bank Y10

Electricity bill

Your company needs to pay for electricity use before you can continue manufacture.

Pay the bank Y5

Rent

Your company's rent is overdue.

Pay the bank Y20

Teamwork commendation

Your company's employees are all working as a team.

Hand in this certificate.

The bank will pay you a Y20 award

Learning Muscles commendation

Your company is demonstrating creative ways of working and good listening.

Hand in this certificate.

The bank will pay you a Y20 award

PHOTOCOPIABLE 12A   Moving to Planet Secon

A new planet, Secon, has been discovered. It has an atmosphere like Earth's. Teams of people have been selected to make the journey to this planet to be new settlers in a new world. It is a one-way journey. Explorers will never be able to return to Earth. It will be too far away. There are four remaining places on the spaceship. Your team's task is to select four people from the list below to take these places. All of them want to go to Secon.

You must agree on your decision unanimously, with reasons for the selection of each individual. Good luck!

1. Kola is an 11-year-old boy, a maths genius. He is an orphan, with a younger sister who is not making the journey.

2. Guy is the richest man on the planet, aged 45. He has a dreadful temper, and is used to getting his own way. He runs a building company, is incredibly practical, and knows exactly how to build homes on the new planet.

3. Josie is a mystic and religious leader, aged 65. She is very quiet and prefers her own company. She is also psychic. She knows about dangers in time for people to prepare against disaster.

4. Shima-Menue, aged 17, is superb at inspiring people to work together. She's great at helping people communicate and sort out their problems. Her parents are not on the expedition. She is their only child. If Shima-Menue joins the trip, it means they will never have grandchildren on Earth.

5. Samir, aged 75, is the world's top expert on plants and animals. He will be able to cope with the plants and animals on the new planet and will supervise taking plants and animals from Earth to Secon. He will leave behind his son, who has been unwell for some time, and two young grandchildren, aged 4 and 6.

6. Sylph is a gifted musician, aged 29, who can play any instrument and read and write music. She alone could take music from Earth to Secon. She would leave behind her elderly mother and a brother who is wheelchair bound after a bad car accident.

7. James is a superb athlete and a doctor. His job would be to teach sports and exercise to the settlers on Secon. He is divorced, with two young children aged 4 and 8 whom he doesn't see as he and his ex-wife do not communicate at all.

8. Yasmin, aged 42, is a gifted teacher and writer. She has researched the teaching of reading and writing and speaks and writes many languages. Her job on Secon would be to share books, reading and writing with settlers.

5. Trust your gut instinct workshops

If there is something we wish to change in the child, we should first examine it and see whether it is not something that could better be changed in ourselves.

Carl Gustav Jung

The prime worry of pupils moving to middle school or secondary school is: 'Will I be safe?' There are lots of other questions. 'Will I fit in? Will I know what to do, when and where? How will I find my way round and be in the right place at the right time? What about bullies? Will I have to join a gang to survive?'

Remember how you felt in the first few weeks of your move to a middle or secondary school. It may be long ago, but for many adults there are still some unpleasant memories. The workshops in this chapter build on listening to your heart by dealing with the basic issue of safety.

Vulnerable pupils – with special needs and/or behavioural issues – need a careful, progressive introduction to their next school. Ensure they meet and bond with a learning mentor and have a peer buddy for at least a month at the start of the new school year. The aim is that they have peers and adults who can help them fit in and assist them with any issues that arise.

Pupils with visual acuity issues need to 'map' their new environment. Staff must be advised of what work format these pupils require in class. They should provide them with a more private place to work in ICT lessons, for which they may need an enlarged screen or to sit very close to the screen. How will design and technology, PE and science investigations be designed to ensure that these children are included in practical work?

Pupils with hearing problems need to be able to see the teachers to lip-read and to have access to signing. Those who have some hearing need to be in classrooms equipped with sound systems to help their learning.

Autistic pupils require careful, slow integration into new situations as change is very frightening for them. Dyspraxic and dyslexic pupils need assistance in organisation. Teachers must understand their needs in the classroom and when setting homework. Pupils working below level 3 in the National Curriculum need enormous support. Gifted and talented pupils need to be challenged in their learning in secondary or middle school or risk becoming disaffected.

How will pupils with mobility issues (with cerebral palsy or wheelchair bound, for instance) access classrooms, corridors, design and technology, and science work areas? Will they have sufficient time to move between subject areas without being frightened and feeling left out? If the new school lacks pupil lockers, how will these pupils carry their bags round during the day? How will they gain access to toilets?

Remember that pupils moving to middle or secondary school are near or experiencing puberty. They are hypersensitive to being 'different' in any way. 'I must fit in' is a mantra for many of them. Special needs pupils may hide their problems, pretend to be OK and begin a dreadful spiral into disaffection or depression. Help them understand that extra help is their entitlement to ensure they have every opportunity they need to learn.

For example, recently a parent told me her Year 10 son who has acute visual problems was provided with GCSE test papers that had not been enlarged to the correct size. Apparently the teachers 'hadn't had time to photocopy them'. This pupil was embarrassed about raising the issue with his parents. He was scared about being 'picked on' by the teachers if he complained. Try to help your special needs parents by giving them links to support groups and information about their children's statutory rights in school.

Check that support arrangements are in place. Involve parents and carers in these meetings. Every pupil has a right to full inclusion. Middle and secondary schools can be large, impersonal institutions where communication failures lead to unnecessary pain and upset for these pupils. Do everything you can to build good relationships with the next school and its staff.

Peer mediator projects

In 2005, Little Ilford Secondary in Newham invited its feeder primaries to list those pupils likely to have problems in making the transition from Year 6 to Year 7 because of behavioural issues. These pupils were asked to attend a week-long summer workshop at Little Ilford run by pastoral care team staff from the school, with workshops designed and run by the Newham Youth Offending Team. Subsequently, all thirty pupils made a successful transition – both socially and in their learning.

A key to the success of this project was that Little Ilford's Year 10 peer mediators – who had received intensive skills training in Year 9 – attended, helped run these workshops and bonded with the incoming pupils. The peer mediators' role within the school was explained to them. They act as go-betweens for issues between pupils: in the playground and elsewhere. Peer mediators often solve the problems with the pupils and those concerned, and only involve other adults when necessary or at a pupil's request.

It is very alarming to read in UK newspapers of children aged 11 to 13 who have committed suicide because of bullying at school. Bullying mobile phone texts and vicious website blog entries have become common weapons, and are as hurtful and evil as physical and verbal abuse.

Ensure that bullying is discussed within this group of workshops and in your class. Above all, children need to know they can talk to someone they trust, and ask for help from an adult when they are bullied or frightened. What is happening is not their fault and they have a right to be safe and to feel good about themselves. Bullying that is not dealt with at the time may cripple people emotionally throughout their lives. One of the guiding principles of this book is to enable pupils to feel strong and good about themselves.

Workshop 14

Goal Setting – Ticket to your Life (1½ hours)

Before you teach this lesson, please use the Ticket to your Life worksheet to set and meet an actual goal for yourself. This is not a lesson you'll find easy to fake.

❍ Learning intention

Pupils understand how they use time in their lives and how to plan to achieve goals.

❍ Success criteria

Pupils can:

- analyse and discuss how effectively they use their time;
- explain how to set a goal and what steps are needed to achieve that goal.

❍ Learning outcome

A Ticket to your Life goal plan for one goal, which they follow through in future lessons and independently.

❍ Resources

Photocopiable 14A (page 81), one for each pupil (possibly two each); Photocopiable 14B (page 82), one for each group; Photocopiable 14C (page 83), one for each pupil; pens or pencils

▷ Introduction (15 minutes)

Give each pupil a copy of Photocopiable 14A to complete for the previous day, allocating hours according to their activities. They could use another copy over the upcoming weekend to highlight their use of time then. Buddy pairs need to be provided for special needs pupils. Dyspraxic pupils or those with difficulty in telling/gauging time need support.

Discuss how much time was used productively and how much was taken by 'time-waster' activities (e.g. television, computer games). How do the pupils define 'productive' and 'time wasting' activities? Does the class agree on the definitions?

▷ Main activity (1 hour)

Give out copies of Photocopiable 14B to groups. Explain that Abraham Maslow designed his original five-stage hierarchy to show how people's goals are determined by the level of life at which they are operating. Here are some examples:

- Refugees escaping from a war zone seek food, shelter and sleep (biological or survival needs). Once they have those, they also seek safety.

- If you are a child who has a home and can move around safely in the world, then you'll focus on having friends and family relationships (belonging needs).

- If those are OK, then you can deal with respect of/for others (esteem needs)

- If you feel good about yourself and others, then you focus on self-actualisation – personal growth and creativity.

What Maslow expressed was that someone operating at the lower levels may find it very difficult to think about levels further up the hierarchy as they have to focus on getting the basics met. It's hard for a pupil to study 'to be their best' (self-actualisation) or be a good friend (belonging) if they have nothing to eat at home because there is no money for food (biological) or because they fear bullies in the playground or on the way to and from school (safety needs). Ask pupils to consider their level of operation regarding transition.

Give out copies of Photocopiable 14C. This workshop is about completion of the ticket to your life and achieving the goal set out. Model goal-setting to your class, using a real goal you've set and met.

The example I gave my classes was saving a deposit for a car. I set a time limit, an amount per month, for a goal of saving £5,000 as a car deposit. It was for a particular make and model of new car and by a set date. As often happens with accurate goal-setting, I achieved that goal early and bought the car. Next, I set up another goal, to pay the car loan. I had a magazine photograph of my car pinned on the wall of my study, with the numbers 1 to 36 written on the car to denote my three-year car loan payments. When I made a monthly payment I crossed off the number. Paying off the car loan became a pleasant game with a serious undertone, and the months appeared to fly by. My classes also saw the car itself, in the car park, so they knew it was a real goal. Take the pupils through your SMART goal.

- The goal itself must be specific – not 'fuzzy'. A fuzzy goal would be 'I want to save some money to buy something next year.' A specific goal is 'I will save £5,000 at £500 a month in 10 months, starting from April 2002, to have the deposit to purchase a Toyota Yaris 1.3 T Spirit in January 2003.' Yep, that exact. Fuzzy goals go nowhere. (It must also have steps to reach the endpoint.)

- It must be measurable – note that I have the amount to save per month, the total number of months and the start and end dates for my goal.

- It must be Attainable, Achievable and Acceptable. You have to want the goal, it must be a goal that is not illegal or immoral and it must be one you can achieve. 'I will buy a lottery ticket each week for ten weeks to win a million pounds for Christmas' isn't attainable or achievable. I really wanted to buy that car, and it was a goal I could reach.

- SMART goals are also realistic. My goal was to purchase a car that would be available when I was ready to purchase it. I set monthly savings targets that I could meet. I already had a driver's licence!

- SMART goals are timed. Note that my goal had specific start and end dates and was clear about what I had to do each month for ten months. What was amazing was that the saving became easier, so I was able to save more and achieve the goal early. If you don't time each step towards your goal, you won't have markers to check how you're doing. Yes, if situations change you can change the achievement date for your goal and what you do at each step. Having a SMART goal gives control and ability to check along the way.

Visualise the goal (10 minutes)

Tell the children:

Sit comfortably, close your eyes and imagine you have a ticket to your life in your hands. On this ticket is one goal you really want to achieve. Run a little film in your head where you look at this ticket and can see what the goal will be.

- Think about one part of your life (one you saw in your time graph) that you want to improve.

- Think about the Maslow pyramid. Where are you now on that pyramid? What do you want to improve? Is it being safe, being a good friend? What else?

- See that part of your life where you want to set one small goal. See yourself achieving the goal so you improve that part of your life. Imagine what you must do, step by step, to reach the goal. See yourself doing this.

- Picture yourself as having achieved the goal. Breathe in and out. Feel how good it is, to have that goal.

- Check. Is this a goal you can measure? Can you see each step on the way? If there are too many steps, is the goal too big? If so, make a smaller goal, with smaller steps to it.

- Can you see it really happening? Do you want it to happen?

- Imagine a calendar in front of you. How many weeks or months will it take you to achieve the goal? If it is a very big, very long-term goal, think of the first step towards that goal. That will be your mini-goal now.

- Now, look at the ticket again and imagine what must be written on it.

- Open your eyes and sit quietly for a few minutes.

Writing the goal (20 minutes)

Allow the class to work in pairs, with special needs or vulnerable pupils having sympathetic helpers, to complete their goal sheet. Some special needs pupils may use pictures to show their goal. Pupils work in pairs to write their goals and steps. Share the goals and ask the class to help people make them more SMART, if needed. Ensure that the goals set are acceptable and realistic. If children do not want to share the goal, that is fine. Arrange for them to have a private time to go through this goal with you, after the lesson.

▷ Plenary (15 minutes)

Talk about how pupils can use pictures from magazines and newspapers to make a small treasure map to remind them of their goal. How will they keep their treasure map and ticket safe? Some children won't be able to take them home. Have a safe place in the classroom that is both private and accessible so they may check their goals.

Ask your class how the Performance Monster may work to sabotage their achieving the goal – explain that it is a challenge and Performance Monsters are terrified of challenges. Keep a list of 'goal killers'. Agree as a class how you will monitor the goals regularly, ticking off each step met, and giving pupils time to amend their goal if necessary. How will you celebrate achieving the goals, as a class? Let the pupils make suggestions and use them.

Organise yourself (1 hour)

This workshop is often run on Year 7 pupil induction days. I've expanded it to include 'What if' activities. It can be attempted for use in a variety of situations.

❍ Learning intention

Pupils understand how they have to organise themselves going to and from and within secondary (or middle) school during the school week.

❍ Success criteria

Pupils can:

- understand and discuss the complexities of a secondary timetable;

- suggest ways they can self-organise to ensure they have the materials and books needed for each day of the week (or fortnight, in schools that run a ten-day timetable);

- have strategies for the start of Year 7 and to deal with things that go wrong.

❍ Learning outcome

Pupils know how to pack their school bag each day.

❍ Resources

Photocopiables 15A and 15B (pages 84 and 85), one timetable and one copy of page 85 for each pair of pupils

Prepared envelopes – one per pair of pupils – made from Photocopiable 15C (page 86), plus six blank cards for each pair (for other items they may add)

Examples of the books/equipment (or photographs on large A4 cards) and a school bag pupils would take every day, to demonstrate in the introduction and for use by special needs pupils when they do the exercise

▷ Introduction (10 minutes)

Check the pupils' knowledge of the following. If they have older siblings, they may be familiar with the organisation of their next school:

- Different teachers for each subject and a more complex timetable. Have examples of Year 7 timetables to show them.

- Pupils must keep a diary with their timetable and their notes of their homework in it. Different teachers give homework on the same or different days, for return on set dates.

- Some schools have lockers. Many do not, and their pupils must carry everything they need for each day in their school bag. It's vital they have what they need for that day, so they must know their timetable and the books and equipment to bring. Detentions may result from failure to do this.

- Getting round the school quickly is vital. They will be given a school map and will learn short-cut routes to classrooms, but will be unable to return to their tutor room to pick up books between classes and will often move large distances between buildings.

- How they pay in the school canteen. Some schools take money; some issue cards which pupils top up at the office or at ATM-type machines to pay for meals and snacks.

- Uniform code and keeping your clothes with you. Losing a jumper in a lesson may mean losing it for ever in a school of 1,800 students.

Ask the children to think of everything they will have to remember each day when they attend their next school. Model one day's preparation with pupils and equipment. Model with Photocopiables 15A and 15B rather than using the cards. Have a real bag they need to fill to show them.

▷ Main activity (30 minutes)

Hand out Photocopiables 15A (cut in half) and 15B and an envelope of cards made from Photocopiable 15C to each pair of pupils. Pupils with special needs – especially dyspraxic and dyslexic students – should work in a group with real items and a real bag, with an adult.

The class completes Photocopiable 15B, placing the items from their envelope on the appropriate rucksack.

▷ Plenary (15 minutes)

The pairs report back on what should go in the bag for each day of the week.

Pupils could demonstrate this, using the bag. Ask what they have discovered about organising themselves for the school week. When would they pack their bags for the next day at school? What about bus/train tickets, money, uniform items, a jacket/gloves in winter? Discuss any issues and ask your class to think of ways in which they could organise themselves at home. Some pupils may use Post-it notes, or put up a timetable in their bedroom. What else can they do?

Trust your Gut Instinct and Stay Safe 1 (1½ hours)

❯ Learning intention

Pupils develop strategies to stay safe in their new school.

❯ Success criteria

Pupils:

- can discuss the safety issues they will encounter;
- role-play situations that may occur, with the likely outcomes of different choices;
- use Learning Muscles and win–win strategy assertiveness in role plays;
- know when to be Street Smart (i.e. when to run rather than talk);
- know what to do if they are bullied and where to go for help.

❯ Learning outcome

Pupils are able to be honest about their fears and know how to deal with them.

❯ Resources

Six sets of cards, five of each, each set a different colour, for use in the jigsaw activity

Photocopiable 16A (page 87), one for each pupil. You may choose to display the topic headings on a flipchart or IWB for the plenary discussion

Pens or pencils

▷ Introduction

Explain to the class that the next two workshops are about being safe in secondary or middle school. If anyone becomes concerned or worried during these workshops, they need to let you know.

▷ Main activity

Jigsaw groups: going to and from school (1 hour)

Give each child a copy of Photocopiable 16A for reference. Divide your class into six groups. Explain that each group will be given one topic to discuss. Each group member must make notes on the ideas agreed to share with others. Give each group a set of same-coloured cards. Explain that the pupils stay in their first group for 10 minutes. They will then be separated and will move around five times to share ideas at other tables, a representative from each group being at each table. Each discussion time at a table is about 10 minutes.

Topics

1. **What should you take to school?**

   Should you take mobile phones, MP3 players, iPods, CDs or DVDs to lend to friends or a large amount of money? Should you wear expensive jewellery to your new school? If not, why not?

2. **Commuting to and from school**

   What about getting to and from your new school? Have you thought about the journey? What about the journey in winter? If you commute from rural areas, will you have a seat on the bus? What time will you leave home and return? Will you need to carry an extra snack or a book for the bus? How will you stay safe on the journey? What if the bus/train is late? Do you have another route home? How can you call home if you have problems? Should you take short cuts that may be dangerous?

3. **Staying after school**

   What about staying after school for clubs or sports, or to hang around? Is that a good idea, or not? Why? If an after-school activity is cancelled and pupils make their own way home, is that a time to go exploring or to have an adventure your parents or carers don't know about? Why? Why not?

4. **Dangers**

   How likely is it that you may be mugged? Who might be the muggers?
   What about strangers, or older students who want to befriend you? Is that too cool to turn down? Should you carry a weapon for defence?
   What if new school friends suggest you bunk off school for the day and go into town, or to the cinema? Good idea? Bad idea? Why?

5. **Bullies**

   If you are bullied in your new school, what should you do? Will you go to a peer mediator, tutor, learning mentor, teacher or parent; or will you be embarrassed and afraid to do that? What steps should you take to deal with bullying? Why don't pupils ask for help when bullied? What about cyber-bullying? (emails / mobile phone texts / blogs on websites)? What if your old friends bully you?

6. **Friends and gangs**

   Would you join a gang to be safe? Would you join if your old friends from primary or new friends in secondary asked you to join? What would you do if you discovered you had to steal from a shop or beat up someone to become a gang member? Would you watch someone in your gang hurt someone? Are gangs cool? If your gang thinks it's not cool to learn in class, would you follow their behaviour? Why do children join gangs?

Note for the teacher:
Young Voice research involving over 7,000 11-year-old pupils in 2003 found that 40 per cent had considered joining gangs and 31 per cent knew someone who carried a weapon for protection. (Young Voice research, *Young Voice Matters*, Issue 1 'Transitions Within Transition', available with *The Big Change* video of children talking about the move from primary to secondary school, from www.young-voice.org)

▷ Plenary

Bring the groups back to their original tables. Ask what they discovered when they shared their points of view about their topic with representatives of other groups round the room. Did they find common concerns? What were they? What did they discover about the issues? What practical skills do they need to deal with these issues? List them. Note that in the next workshop, the group will role-play how to deal with issues under each of these topics. Perhaps prior to the next workshop they could ask older siblings how they've dealt with these issues. Make notes on flipchart paper to use in the next workshop.

Finally, check if possible whether they were honest about their fears and worries or trying to be cool. Encourage them to consider the danger of being cool.

▷ Additional support: ICT or P4C lesson(s)

Direct pupils to the websites that offer information about bullying and transfer to secondary school: www.kidscape.org.uk (resources for pupils on bullying); www.needtoknow.co.uk/beatbullying and www.childline.org.uk/extra/bullyingindex.asp. Search these websites yourself. There is excellent information on how to identify and deal with cyber-bullying. Do you need to run an ICT lesson that focuses on being safe on the Internet to avoid becoming subject to this kind of bullying?

You may wish to use some of the leaflets or poems from the DfES National Anti-Bullying Poetry Competition publication (www.dfes.gov.uk/bullying) as stimuli for P4C sessions. Do this prior to the next workshop.

Trust your Gut Instinct and Stay Safe 2 (1½ hours)

○ Learning intention

Pupils develop strategies to stay safe in their new school.

○ Success criteria

Pupils:

- can discuss the safety issues they will encounter;
- role-play situations that may occur, with likely outcomes of different choices;
- use Learning Muscles and win–win strategy assertiveness in role-plays;
- know when to be Street Smart (i.e. when to run rather than talk);
- know what to do if they are bullied and where to go for help;
- can be honest about their fears and know how to deal with them.

This workshop follows on directly from Workshop 16. The pupils have discussed the staying safe ideas. Hopefully, you've explored the websites and shared anti-bullying information, including guidelines on how to deal with cyber-bullying. Perhaps you've used some of the anti-bullying poems from the DfES website already mentioned.

○ Resources

Young Voice video *The Big Change* from www.young-voice.org

Cards made from Photocopiable 17A (page 88), one set of a theme for each group

A Trust your Gut Emotionometer – a long line you draw on an IWB or flipchart, with 0 at one end and 10 at the other. You may decide to keep a master copy of this on a flipchart for pupils to use in the future.

▷ Introduction

You need to work in a hall or large work space.

Show *The Big Change* video and encourage the pupils to note how positively these pupils present secondary school. What if it isn't all rosy and wonderful? How do we deal with the issues we discussed in our groups in the last workshop?

Remind the pupils of the assertiveness techniques (win–win) from previous workshops. Ask them to list what skills are needed to solve conflicts. They should cover these:

- Assertive listening, in which you check the other person's understanding of the issue, rather than making your own assumptions.

- Win–win communication: strong body language and voice, not aggressive; use of fogging and self-assertion; agreement where you are in the wrong.

- Knowing when to be Street Smart and get away from a situation without apology or explanation.

Explain that they will prepare role-plays in groups and perform them. The class will then help them solve the problems or suggest ways to help.

Main activity

Organise groups of 6 so that vulnerable and shy children have an adult or buddy to support them in the activity. Give safety guidelines and emphasise no violence or swearing in role-plays – explain they may mime it, rather than doing it. If a child feels unsafe, they may call 'stop' and the group must stop immediately.

Hand out cards made from Photocopiable 17A, one for each member of each group, with their role-play activity written on them. You may make additional cards showing situations that you know are particularly appropriate. Pupils talk about the issues, and role-play the scene with two endings – the student chooses a good outcome and a dangerous outcome. Rehearse to show the class.

Pupils rehearse and perform the role-play scenes, with both endings. The class then plays 'talking statues' with the actors. If they think of a better end to the scene, they stop the actors, suggest an alternative and the actors role-play that new ending.

 ## Plenary

Discuss the role-play scenes. Are children able to tell when they should stay and talk and when they should use their Street Smart skills and leave? Discuss other issues that come up. What strategies do they already have to deal with these issues? What do they need to learn? How can they ensure they seek help if they encounter any bullying? What is the danger of needing to be cool or fit in, when the situation is threatening? Is peer pressure an excuse for bad behaviour? Invite pupils to speak to you after the session, or in future lessons, if they feel worried or concerned about the issues raised.

Display a Trust your Gut Instinct Emotionometer. State that 0 indicates issues that pupils can deal with by themselves and 10 issues that they know they need to ask for help with. Ask the class to rate all the dangers and worries of the move to secondary school and place them and the role-plays on the emotionometer. Give the pupils cards and pens and use Blu-Tack® to display their cards on the emotionometer. Allow pupils to discuss how cards could be moved further up or down the line and agree the final placement on the line, as a class.

Contain the emotions in this plenary. Do not underestimate the power of the fears and monsters you've let loose in the classroom. Note that when we become very excited or angry, our reptilian brain takes over control and it can take hours to return to a normal state in which we can take in any information and function as usual.

This is why we shouldn't argue with an enraged student, and should give ourselves time to recover whenever we are angry or upset. For example, if we have an argument before or after school, it can affect the rest of our day. The role-plays involve high emotions, so end this session with a quiet centring activity. Remind pupils how to return to a calm state after they've been angry or upset.

 ## Follow-up activities

- Ground the learning of these last two workshops by involving theatre groups, activities in your PSHE and SEAL programmes, and further practice of win–win skills.

- Put the monster in a box or boxes! Ask pupils to take all their fears and anger about secondary school, draw it as a monster, then make the monster from scrap materials. During the last weeks in school, have a ceremony in which pupils make a short speech about their secondary scares monster (or Performance Monster) and then stomp it into oblivion. I used this activity in Year 6 for many years to create SATs monsters. The destruction ceremony is very impressive!

- Pupils can create murals or sculptures of win–win situations, or write poems or plays/stories for Year 5 pupils moving into Year 6 the next year.

- They can create musical compositions and dance that demonstrate dealing with bullying and dangers in secondary: raps, songs, dance stories, drumming and percussion pieces. Encourage them to make it real!

- Use other team games and activities to practise team communication and work skills.

Suggested list of activities to use

Devise a symbol for each entry.

School time

Looking after myself: bathroom, hair, teeth

Sleep

Homework

Serious hobbies outside school time: sports, language lessons, music

Play-time outside school: time with friends, visiting relatives

Time by myself: reading, computer, thinking about stuff

TV time: in my room or with the family

Phone time: talking and texting

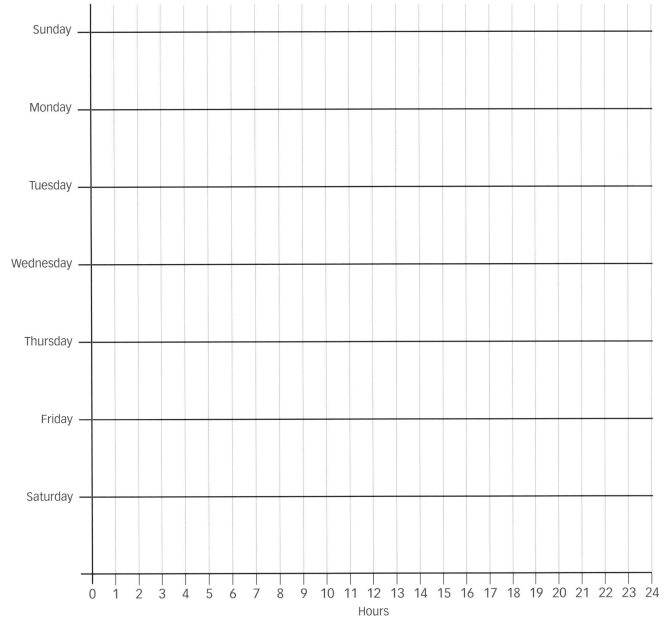

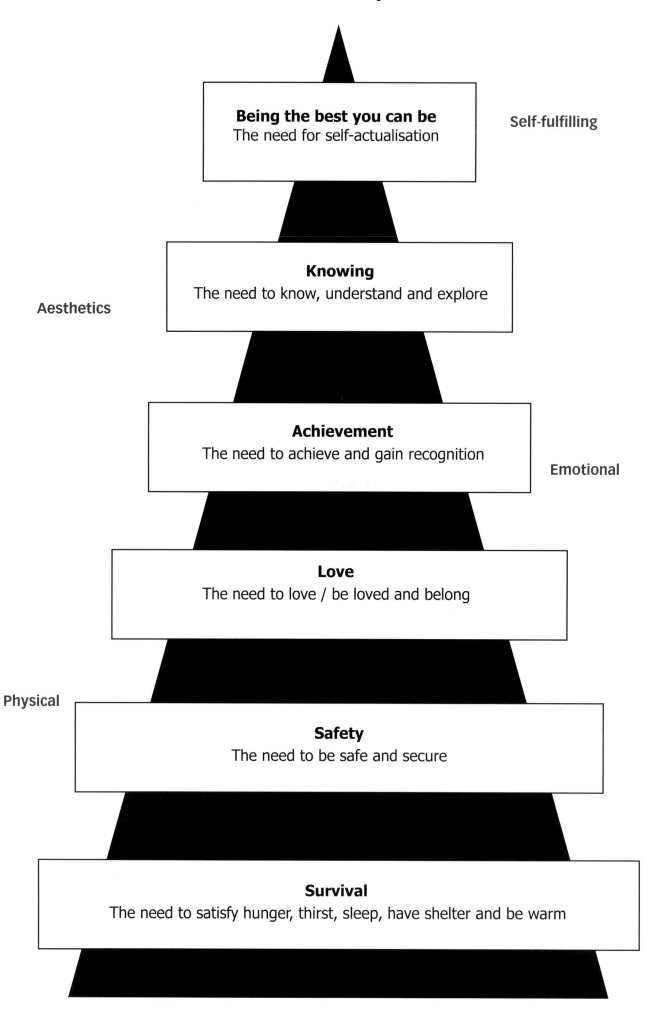

Being the best you can be
The need for self-actualisation

Self-fulfilling

Knowing
The need to know, understand and explore

Aesthetics

Achievement
The need to achieve and gain recognition

Emotional

Love
The need to love / be loved and belong

Physical

Safety
The need to be safe and secure

Survival
The need to satisfy hunger, thirst, sleep, have shelter and be warm

PHOTOCOPIABLE 14C   Ticket to your Life

Name...

Date of departure ....Date of arrival at goal...

My goal...

S Specific goal: Write exactly what you want to achieve, when you will start and finish, and how many steps are in the journey.

M Measure your goal: List each *step* you will need to take to reach your goal and exactly what you must do at each step.

1. ....

2. ....

3. ....

4. ....

5. ....

A Is this goal Attainable, Achievable and Acceptable? How do you know you can do it? Who will be pleased when you reach the goal? What will you do when you arrive at your goal? Is this goal right for you and good for you? Will it cause no harm to yourself or others?

R Is this a Realistic goal? What other goal like this have you attained? What have you already done towards this goal?

T Timed. Are you certain you will check and tick each step on your goal plan (measure) and amend it if necessary? When will you do this?

When you have completed this form and discussed it with a partner and your teacher, ask them to sign it with you.

I... [*your name*] **am now starting my journey to my goal.** I will check each as I work to my goal and talk about any problems with my partner or teacher.

....(signature) ....(partner's signature)

....(teacher's signature) ....(date)

PHOTOCOPIABLE 15A   Secondary/Middle School Timetable

Session	Monday	Tuesday	Wednesday	Thursday	Friday
1.	Maths	Maths	English	Geography	Maths
2.	English	Geography	Science	PE	Music
3.	History	Drama	French	English	RE
4.	PE	English	PSHE	Science	English
5.	Technology	PE	History	Art	Science
6.	French	Science	ICT	Maths	Technology

Session	Monday	Tuesday	Wednesday	Thursday	Friday
1.	Maths	Maths	English	Geography	Maths
2.	English	Geography	Science	PE	Music
3.	History	Drama	French	English	RE
4.	PE	English	PSHE	Science	English
5.	Technology	PE	History	Art	Science
6.	French	Science	ICT	Maths	Technology

                    Permission to Photocopy

Monday

Tuesday

Wednesday

Thursday

Friday

PHOTOCOPIABLE 15C Stuff-to-bring Cards

ENGLISH Exercise book for 1st lesson of week	Diary planner Tuesday	ENGLISH Exercise book for 4th lesson of week	MATHS Exercise book Homework for 4th lesson of week	TECHNOLOGY Exercise book for 2nd lesson of week	PE KIT (athletics) for 3rd lesson of week
ICT Homework exercise due 1 day before lesson	Pencil case Wednesday	ENGLISH Exercise book Homework for 3rd lesson of week	MATHS Calculator for 4th lesson of week	ENGLISH Exercise book for 5th lesson of week	SCIENCE Exercise book for 1st lesson of week
HISTORY Exercise book for 2nd lesson of week	MUSIC Homework book	Pencil case Friday	Book for library: due back Monday	ENGLISH Homework Exercise book for 2nd lesson of week	MATHS Exercise book Homework for 2nd lesson of week
FRENCH Homework Exercise book for 2nd lesson of week	SCIENCE Exercise book Homework for last lesson of week	GEOGRAPHY Exercise book for 2nd lesson of week	SCIENCE Exercise book for 2nd lesson of week	MATHS Calculator for 1st lesson of week	Pencil case Tuesday
MATHS Exercise book Homework for 1st lesson of week	SCIENCE Exercise book Homework for 3rd lesson of week	TECHNOLOGY Equipment for 1st lesson of week	MUSIC Exercise book	PE KIT (games) for 2nd lesson of week	FRENCH Dictionary for 1st lesson of week
Letter for trip: return on Tuesday	Memory stick for ICT lesson	MATHS Exercise book Textbook for Thursday	GEOGRAPHY Homework Exercise book for 1st lesson of week	RE Homework folder Exercise book	ICT Folder Homework book
MATHS Calculator for 3rd lesson of week	HISTORY Exercise book Homework for 1st lesson of week	MATHS Calculator for 2nd lesson of week	Pencil case Monday	PE KIT (swimming) for 1st lesson of week	Diary planner Monday
Diary planner Wednesday	Diary planner Thursday	Diary planner Friday	ART Sketch book	Pencil case Thursday	Pay money / top-up card for lunch, Monday

PHOTOCOPIABLE 16A Trust your Gut Instinct and Stay Safe

Discuss the topic you are given in your group. Make notes on the back of this sheet to share when you move to other groups.

1. What should you take to school?

Should you take mobile phones, MP3 players, iPods, CDs or DVDs to lend to friends or a large amount of money? Should you wear expensive jewellery to your new school? If not, why not?

2. Commuting to and from school

What about getting to and from your new school? Have you thought about the journey? What about the journey in winter? If you commute from rural areas, will you have a seat on the bus? What time will you leave home and return? Will you need to carry an extra snack or a book for the bus? How will you stay safe on the journey? What if the bus/train is late? Do you have another route home? How can you call home if you have problems? Should you take short cuts that may be dangerous?

3. Staying after school

What about staying after school for clubs or sports or to hang around? Is that a good idea, or not? Why? If an activity is cancelled and pupils make their own way home, is that a time to explore or have an adventure your parents or carers don't know about? Why? Why not?

4. Dangers

How likely is it that you may be mugged? Who might be the muggers?

What about strangers, or older students who want to befriend you? Is that too cool to turn down? Should you carry a weapon for defence?

What if new school friends suggest you bunk off school for the day and go into town, or to the cinema? Good idea? Bad idea? Why?

5. Bullies

If you are bullied in your new school, what should you do? Will you go to a peer mediator, tutor, learning mentor, teacher or parent; or will you be embarrassed and afraid to do that? What steps should you take to deal with bullying? Why don't pupils ask for help when bullied? What about cyber-bullying? (emails / mobile phone texts / blogs on websites) What if your old friends bully you?

6. Friends and gangs

Would you join a gang to be safe? Would you join if your old friends from primary or new friends in secondary asked you to join? What would you do if you discovered you had to steal from a shop or beat up someone to become a gang member? Would you watch someone in your gang hurt someone? Are gangs cool? If your gang thinks it's not cool to learn in class, would you follow their behaviour? Why do children join gangs?

PHOTOCOPIABLE 17A Trust your Gut Instinct and Stay Safe Role-plays

1. What should you take to school?

Your new best friend at secondary school asks you to bring your iPod to school for her to borrow. She then claims she's lost it, but other pupils tell you she's taken it home. What do you do?

2. Commuting to and from school

Your bus doesn't turn up. You've spent your phone money on food. You want to get home, but your family thinks you're at a cancelled after-school sports club and aren't expecting you for two hours. What do you do? What could go wrong?

3. Staying after school

You told your family you're seeing a friend after school, on the way home. They don't know that the only adults in the house are their older brothers who like to smoke weed and drink. They invite you to join in. What do you do? What happens?

4. Dangers

You're walking to the bus stop, it's dark and your bus isn't due for 15 minutes. Three older boys approach you, hold a knife at you and ask for your mobile phone, your money and your baseball cap. It's a new phone, you've only got money for the bus and you really love the baseball cap. What do you do? What happens? What do you learn from this experience?

5. Bullies

You're being bullied. It's cunning. You're sent foul text messages. Someone is putting up evil blogs on a website, you have had threatening phone calls. The bullies push you in the corridors and call you names. You have no friends to confide in and you don't know who exactly is orchestrating the bullying. They've said if you tell anyone, they'll get you. What do you do?

6. Friends and gangs

Your best mate from primary school, or new best friends at secondary – or people you'd really like to be your friends because they're popular and cool – ask you to join their gang. There's a catch. You have to prove you're cool enough to join by doing some despicable things. You have to be cruel and sarcastic to a special needs pupil in your year, steal clothes from a list you're given from the local stores, be rude to teachers, never criticise the gang members and then – they tell you – you have to mug two 5-year-olds in the street. What do you do?

6. Transition as a whole-school Issue

A mind, once stretched by a new idea never regains its original dimension

Oliver Wendell Holmes Junior

Workshops for parents, staff and governors

Primary to secondary (or middle) school transition affects everyone in your school's community. Involving parents, governors and staff enables the process to be better understood. It also ensures you can bring people 'on board' with plans for projects and school links.

What you can do

Read through the workshops in Chapters 3, 4 and 5 and decide which ones you'd like to run with parents or carers and other adults present, to assist and be involved.

Workshop 8 (Stepping Stones in Life) and Workshop 11 (Money Shapes Game) in Chapter 4 would be great fun for adults, either helping in class or in an after-school session for parents and carers.

Adapt Stepping Stones in Life (page 40) and ask the adults to consider a major transition in their lives that the two activities in this workshop bring back to them. Let them consider what the transition was, what happened, how they felt before and after the transition and how it changed them. When they have shared these experiences, let them consider how transition between schools is a major change for their children.

The Money Shapes game (page 48) can be adapted as a school-fund raiser, as well as being run exactly as designed. Let children be the organisers, once they understand the game!

Workshop 14 (Goal Setting – Ticket to your Life) from Chapter 5 (page 70) may be run as a staff Inset, or as part of staff peer coaching, with teachers and support staff setting personal goals and supporting each other in their attainment.

Similarly, Workshop 2 (Performance Monster and Learning Muscles) in Chapter 3 (page 14) makes a fascinating staff Inset. Many adults have areas of their lives in which Performance Monsters reign. I found this one of the most powerful Insets I ran with staff.

How to move forward as a school

Photocopiable 18A is a primary and secondary Year 6–Year 7 audit which the senior management of your school may complete to gain a picture of your school's current situation and developmental points. Sample transition policies (primary and secondary) from Newham schools follow. They show how some schools involved in a long-term transition project have built transition considerations into their whole school ethos.

Begin small and develop links with your local primary schools as a cluster, then invite your secondaries or middle schools to join you in initial projects. Keep it simple and small scale, build the relationships, build the bridges.

School: _____

No. of Y6 pupils: _____

No. of Y7 pupils: _____

	✓	✗	Next steps
Bridge 1: Bureaucratic – HOW IS INFORMATION TRANSFERRED?			
1. Established LA/borough procedures for transferring pupil files to next school			
2. Clear lines of communication for information transfer			
3. Common induction day for all pupils in LA/borough			
4. SEN and cared-for children final reviews done, files transferred and checked. Suggest set-up in new school			
5. Secondary/middle schools have common information form for primaries, help to support completion			
6. School has transition co-ordinator and transition policy			
7. Parents know how to complete and submit forms correctly and help is available to achieve this			
Bridge 2: Social and Personal – PUPILS & PARENTS PREPARED			
1. Parents and pupils well informed about schools and choices			
2. Effective parents' meetings organised and linked to middle/secondary school			
3. Pupil peer mentoring systems run in school and linked to next school			
4. Adult mentor support for vulnerable pupils set up and monitored regularly			
5. Staff from primary and secondary/middle school support vulnerable parents/carers			
6. Joint social events (beyond induction days) run between Y5/Y6 and Y7			
7. Pupil-voice and pupil project visits between primary and secondary/middle			
Bridge 3: Curricular – CURRICULUM/LEARNING CONTINUITY			
1. Teachers in each phase understand respective assessment, pupil-tracking and target-setting processes			
2. Learning-based cross-phase teaching and learning projects in core subjects			
3. Teachers visit and work in classes in other phases, plan lessons together			
4. Know how each phase supports learning for SEN, gifted and talented, and challenging pupils			
5. Saturday schools, Y5/Y6 classes in secondary, holiday schools and projects			
6. Shared parental Insets: learning expectations, homework skills, learning skills			
7. Pupils' portfolios: writing samples, ICT, subject primary/secondary transition units transferred			
Bridge 4: CONTINUITY OF TEACHING PEDAGOGY AND PRACTICE			
1. Subject co-ordinators work in secondary/middle school to share pedagogy and practice			
2. Cross-phase team teaching, planned together, sharing ways of teaching and learning are timetabled in schools			
3. Shared cross-phase teacher training occurs: Insets, conferences, borough subject forums			
4. Cross-phase meta-cognitive skills and cross-curricular projects, pupils transfer ideas between subjects			
5. Shared teacher use and understanding of AfL in both phases			
6. LA/borough consultants/advisers encourage and lead cross-phase projects with schools			
Bridge 5: MANAGEMENT OF LEARNING (children own their learning)			
1. Pupils understand their preferred ways of learning and stuff they like to do, build Learning Muscles			
2. Parents'/carers' Insets to support children as independent, self-reflective learners			
3. Pupils self-assess, peer-assess and own their learning, reflect on progress: techniques shared cross-phase			
4. Support skills training for pupils with SEN, gifted and talented, behavioural needs, so they own learning			

Permission to Photocopy

Tollgate Primary, London Borough of Newham, recognises that education should be an unbroken continuum whereby all children have a successful and smooth transfer to their chosen secondary school.

Aims

The aims of the transition policy are consistent with the Five Bridges involved in transition:

- Bureaucratic – to ensure the proper documentation is available on transfer.

- Social – to identify and target specific support for those students considered to be vulnerable who have difficulty making the transition to secondary school.

- Curricular – to ensure curriculum continuity by knowledge of the Year 7 core curriculum subjects, cross-phase curricular activities and completing transition units.

- Pedagogical – to be able to communicate learning and teaching styles used in Tollgate.

- Management of Learning – to develop students as independent and reflective learners.

The Five Bridges to transition

Bureaucratic

In Tollgate Primary School there is an identified Year 6–7 transition co-ordinator whose job is to liaise with the borough transition co-ordinator and secondary Year 6–7 co-ordinators to ensure a successful transition for all students to secondary school. Alongside the Year 6 teachers the transition co-ordinator will ensure that all proper documentation is passed on to the appropriate school. The documentation includes their SATs papers, yearly reports, tracking files and where necessary past IEPs and child protection files. Tollgate Primary School uses the DfES (DCSF) common transfer file as the main vehicle for transferring information. Where necessary, the inclusion manager and learning mentor will meet their opposite numbers at secondary school to make additional administrative arrangements for transition to meet the needs of specific groups of children, such as those with special educational needs, gifted and talented, students with English as an additional language and those who are deemed 'at risk' or vulnerable.

At all times parents are kept informed of all necessary arrangements for transition such as filling in the forms, the selection process and appeals process, and where necessary meetings are held to help support parents.

Social

Tollgate feels it is important that all students are given the opportunity to experience their new learning environment prior to moving there, so all children are given the chance to visit their new school and specific programmes of transition are set up for children where appropriate. These visits begin in Year 5, when the children have an opportunity to have a taster day at Tollgate's main feeder school. When the students are in Year 6 they all attend either a day or half-day induction. Secondary inclusion managers are also invited to annual reviews for students with special educational needs; they attend the review, meet the student and set up additional visits for the student.

Curricular and pedagogical

To ensure the continuity of the curriculum between Year 6 and Year 7, cross-key-stage links are encouraged, whereby secondary teachers are invited to come into Tollgate and work with the Year 6 children and their teachers. This is done in the form of observations, secondary teachers teaching the Year 6 children, or doing a combined project with a specific secondary school. Reciprocal visits are encouraged by Tollgate's Year 6 teachers, to visit the local secondary schools. Year 6 teachers are encouraged to have an understanding of the Year 7 curriculum. Students in Year 6 complete the transition units of work, which are to be continued in secondary school. All our teachers are made aware of key national initiatives such as Every Child Matters and Assessment for Learning, which ensure the students have continuity within the curriculum.

Management of learning

Tollgate ensures that its students are seen as active participants in the transition process and in their own learning. Year 6 students are encouraged to take more responsibility for their own learning and to reflect on what they have achieved. Students are encouraged to participate in discussions related to the transition to secondary school and to share their feelings or any concerns they may have. This will help the students to be more confident and independent as they embark on their secondary school life.

Little Ilford transition policy

We acknowledge that having a successful transition system in place will help to allay concerns of students coming to Little Ilford Secondary, London Borough of Newham, and reduce the impact of change on student progress and development.

Our aim is to ensure that students are given the opportunity to make the social and academic transition successfully. To do this we need to:

a) ensure that we have a robust administrative process for collecting and transferring student data as accurately as possible;

b) have a clear understanding of the role of staff and parents in the transition process;

c) establish and maintain active and ongoing working links with our partner primaries;

d) provide opportunities for students and parents to become familiar with Little Ilford so that they are aware of the curriculum offered and the pastoral support available;

e) ensure students are active participants in the transition process and in their own learning.

How?

Administrative bridge

Meetings with key school staff in partner primaries to set dates for transition team to:

- meet class teachers

- collect transferring information

- collect portfolios of work.

SEN staff visit each primary school to gather information on students who have special educational needs.

Social bridge

Preparing families for transition

Transition co-ordinator attends partner primary parents' meetings to distribute prospectuses, answer questions and give information about Little Ilford School; for example:

- curriculum on offer

- support during transition.

All primary parents are invited to our open evening, with this focus:

- Our values and beliefs

- How we maximise every student's potential

- Support structures in place, for example:

    - peer mentoring

    - anti-bullying

    - pastoral support

    - PSHE and citizenship

    - our general expectations.

In June, we have a parents' evening for our new intake – parents have the opportunity to meet staff and students have the opportunity to meet tutors.

In October, a Year 7 settling-in evening is held to evaluate the effectiveness of the transition process.

The transition programme is overseen by an assistant head teacher. The transition co-ordinator and their team are responsible for effective administrative arrangements and providing induction/intervention programmes for relevant students, which will include a summer school.

Curriculum bridge

We use prior attainment information in a proactive way to project outcomes for each student throughout Key Stage 3. We expect each child to progress at least 1.6 levels from their Key Stage 2 results; for example, if a student has a Level 3A in their Key Stage 2 English we would expect them to attain Level 5B in their Key Stage 3 SATs examination.

Progress is assessed on their current and potential grade/level of achievement. Students who are below national expectations participate in a variety of intervention programmes. The information is shared with staff, who use it to inform their lesson planning. In addition, we assess student progress several times a year. Information on each student's progress is shared with each parent during the academic review day.

Through visits to primary schools and teaching, our staff will gain an understanding of the Key Stage 2 curriculum and how it is taught. They will build up exemplar portfolios of students' work for each level by having moderation meetings with primary school staff.

This information is cascaded through departments so that others have an understanding of the standards and expectations of Key Stage 2 students – cluster activities enable team-teaching to take place. Joint transition projects also occur.

At Little Ilford we make additional curriculum arrangements for transition to meet the needs of specific groups such as those students with special education needs, gifted and talented, students with English as an additional language, and those students who are performing below national expectations. All students who gained a Level 3 in their Key Stage 2 English SATs examination will be on a literacy progress unit, which offers small-group teaching to enable the student to progress to Level 4 and beyond. Students may also do the reading challenge, which offers students one-to-one support with their reading.

Pedagogical bridge

The transition co-ordinator and appropriate staff, through a series of visits and team-teaching, will have an understanding of the primary student's approaches to learning and teaching.

Our advanced skills teachers in art and drama support primary school teachers in the teaching of art and drama.

The school sports co-ordinator works with our partner primaries to develop PE in their schools. Through the junior sports leaders award, the school sport co-ordinator trains up primary teachers to teach PE lessons. The transition co-ordinator's major aim is to maximise the learning and teaching methods in primary school classes to inform the practice of teachers at Little Ilford, particularly Year 7 teaching.

Our focus is on active and engaging learning using a variety of teaching activities. We extend and enhance this practice in order that all students have full access and are actively engaged in their learning.

Lessons are observed by the senior leadership team to ensure consistency of practice.

Management of learning

Transition process

Students are empowered to take part in and develop the transition process proactively. Year 7 children visit Year 6 and Year 5 children and discuss their experiences of transition.

In addition, we offer the learning challenge to students who have difficulty with their personal organisation, so that they can manage themselves more effectively. Students below Level 2 receive small-class support with their reading.

Year 7 students feed back their learning experiences to the senior leadership team.

Learning styles

Through a variety of activities in lessons, we try to meet students' particular learning styles, which enables students to progress.

Developing reflective learners

A PSHE session requires students to reflect actively upon their experiences around transition.

We have a praise postcard system which celebrates positive qualities including learning.

Students are encouraged to talk about learning on a regular basis so that they understand the language of learning.

References

Cave, Kathryn and Chris Riddell: *Something Else* (London: Puffin, 1995)

Dawes, Lyn, Neil Mercer & Rupert Wegerif: *Thinking Together: a Programme of Activities for Developing Thinking Skills at KS2* (Birmingham: Questions, 2004)

Dawrent, Ainsley: Building More Bridges: The Newham Y6–Y7 Transition Project, 2004–2006, End of Project Report (www.secondary.newham.gov.uk under Secondary Networks)

De Bono, Edward: *Teach your Child How to Think* (London: Penguin, 1994)

DfES: *Curriculum Continuity: Effective Transfer between Primary and Secondary Schools*, KS3 National Strategy Guidance (DfES 0116-2004G)

Dweck, Carol: *Self Theories: Their Role in Motivation, Personality and Development* (Philadelphia: Taylor & Francis, 2000)

Edwards, Betty: *Drawing on the Right Side of the Brain* (New York: Tarcher, 1989)

Fisher, Robert: *Games for Thinking* (Oxford: Nash Pollock, 1997)

Galton, Maurice, John Gray & Jean Rudduck: *Transfer and Transitions in the Middle Years of Schooling (7–14): Continuities and Discontinuities in Learning* (Research Report RR443, DfES, 2003)

Gardner, Howard: *Frames of Mind* (New York: Basic Books, 1993)

Gardner, Howard: *Intelligence Reframed* (New York: Basic Books, 1999)

Grant, Joan & Neil Curtis: *Cat and Fish* (Melbourne, Australia: Lothian, 2003)

Jeffers, Oliver: *Lost and Found* (London: HarperCollins Children's Books, 2005)

Kübler-Ross, Elisabeth: *On Death and Dying* (London: Macmillan, 1969)

Layton, George: *The Fib and Other Stories* (London: Macmillan 1997)

Mosley, Jenny & Marilyn Tew: *Quality Circle Time in the Secondary School* (London: David Fulton Publishers, 1999)

Seuss, Theodor: *Oh, the Places you'll Go!* (New York: Random House, 1990)

Seuss, Theodor: *Oh, the Thinks you'll Think!* (New York: Random House, 1987)

Stanley, Sara: *Creating Inquiring Minds* (London: Network Continuum, 2006)

Young Voice, *The Big Change Video* (www.young-voice.org)